VELVET

VELVET
History Techniques Fashions

edited by
Fabrizio de' Marinis

essays by
Aurora Fiorentini Capitani
Roberta Orsi Landini
Luisella Pennati
Alfredo Redaelli
Stefania Ricci

IDEA BOOKS

Iconographic Research
Barbara Cattaneo
Véronique Vienne
in collaboration with the authors

Photographic Arrangements at pages
74 - 75 - 110 - 111 - 136 - 137 - 143 - 167 -
169 - 171 - 173 - 175 - 177 - 179 - 193
by Pietro Carrieri

Coordination
Angela Passigli

Art Director
Mario Piazza

Lay-out
Simonetta Rocco
Jessica Zanardi
Studio Achilli & Piazza e Associati

English Translation
Antony Shugaar

Editorial Secretary
Laura Bassi

Print and Bound
Conti Tipocolor srl, Florence

Front Cover
Photograph Pietro Carrieri

The publisher and the authors wish to thank
Riccardo, Alfredo Redaelli and Gabriele Valdata
for their kind collaboration.

Idea Books. Inc.
250 West 57th Street
New York. N.Y. 10107

© Copyright 1994
for English edition
© Copyright 1993
Idea Books, Milan
via Vigevano, 41
20144 Milan

Printed in Italy
European
ISBN 88-7017-115-9

United States
ISBN: 0-9627985-1-7

This book has been made possible through the generous support of:
Associazione Cotoniera Milan
Redaelli Velluti, Mandello del Lario

Acknowlegments:

Rita Airaghi, Ufficio Stampa Gianfranco Ferré, Milano; Alfa Romeo, Arese; Archivio Storico del Comune di Todi; Fabienne Auzolle, Servizio Documentazione del Musée du Mobilier National, Parigi; Emanuela Barbieri, D. B. Studio Italia, Milano; Luciano Belli, Assessore alla Cultura del Comune di Spoleto, Spoleto; Feliciano Benvenuti, Venezia; Bianchi & C., Pescara; Patrizia Biffi, Ufficio Stampa del Teatro alla Scala, Milano; Caterina Bon Valsassina, Sovrintendente Beni Artistici e Storici, Perugia; Alessandra Bossi, Museo del Tessuto di Prato, Prato; Bérangère Broman, Ufficio Stampa Christian Lacroix, Parigi; The Brooklyn Museum, New York; Lia Brunati, Ufficio Stampa Romeo Gigli, Milano; Massimo Buconi, Archivio Storico del Comune, Todi; Liana e Carlo Carnevali, Firenze; Giulia Caruso, Ufficio Stampa Romeo Gigli, Milano; Stefano Cashiù, Direttore Sovrintendente dei Beni Artistici e Storici, Arezzo; Valeria Cerni, Ufficio Stampa Krizia, Milano; Bruno Chiaverini, Direttore ERAI (Enterprise Rhone Alpes Int.), Torino; Carla Clerici, Archivio Fotografico del Teatro alla Scala, Milano; Adriana Corbella, Museo Teatrale alla Scala, Milano; Henry-Claude Cousseau, Direttore del Musée des Beaux Arts, Nantes; Patrizia Cucco, Ufficio Stampa Gianni Versace, Milano; Doretta Davanzo Poli, Venezia; Francine Dawans, Sovrintendente del Musée d'Art Moderne, Liegi; Eleonore De Musset, Ufficio Stampa Yves Saint Laurent, Parigi; Nicole De Reynies, Musée du Mobilier National, Parigi; Danielle Decomis, Direttrice del Patrimonio Lanvin, Parigi; Alda, Tito, Vito Di Fabio, Guardiagrele; Gimmo Etro, Milano; Thierry Favre, Firenze; Rossana Fioravanti, Ufficio Edizioni e Archivio Storico del Teatro alla Scala, Milano; Maria Teresa Fiorio, Civiche Raccolte d'Arte Castello Sforzesco, Milano; Fondazione Arte della Seta Lisio, Firenze; Fondazione Mario Praz, Roma; Claudio Franzini, Archivio Fotografico di Palazzo Fortuny, Venezia; Pietro Fredianelli, Sartoria del Teatro alla Scala, Milano; Elena Fumagalli, Archivio Fotografico del Teatro alla Scala, Milano; Silvio Fuso, Direttore del Museo Palazzo Fortuny, Venezia; Galleria del Costume, Firenze; Renato Garavaglia, Responsabile Ufficio Stampa del Teatro alla Scala, Milano; Maddalena Garcea, Ufficio Stampa Gianfranco Ferré, Milano; Giorgia Gherardi, Archivio Fotografico del Museo Civico Medioevale, Bologna; Annie Gilet, Sovrintendente dei Musée de Tours, Tours; Ester Giovachini, COO.RE.C-.T.A. Spoleto; Roberto Guerri, Civiche Raccolte Storiche, Milano; Monique Jay e collaboratori, Biblioteca del Musée Historique des Tissus, Lione; Marie Andrée Jouve, Balenciaga, Parigi; Magnolia Laurenzi, Ufficio Stampa Max Mara, Milano; Michele Lofredo, Archivio Fotografico Sovrintendenza dei Beni Artistici e Storici, Arezzo; Francesco Lullo, Direttore Civica Biblioteca, Guardiagrele; Jacques François Marchandise, Direttore di Editions Plume, Parigi; Massimo Medica, Direttore Museo Civico Medioevale, Bologna; Anna Maria Mesche, Sovrintendente dei Beni Artistici e Storici, Arezzo; Metropolitan Museum of Art, New York; Priscilla Michoud, Ufficio Stampa Givenchy, Parigi; Stefania Moronato, Palazzo Mocenigo, Venezia; Paola Mosi, Cassa di Risparmio, Firenze; Alessandra Mottola, Museo Poldi Pezzoli, Milano; Museo Nacional del Prado, Madrid; Museo di Arte Sacra, Asciano; Museo di Capodimonte, Napoli; Museo Diocesiano, Ascoli Piceno; Museo Napoleonico, Roma; National Gallery, Londra; Palazzo Ducale, Urbino; Chantal Pauwaert, Servizio Cultura Sovrintendenza Memling Museum, Bruge; Anna Pavard, Servizio Fototeca del Musée de l'Armée, Parigi; Silvana Pettenati, Museo Civico di Torino, Torino; Danielle Pinelli, Ufficio Stampa Lanvin, Parigi; Lucia Portoghesi, Museo del Tessuto e del Costume di Spoleto, Roma; Rosangela Procopio, Ufficio Stampa del Teatro alla Scala, Milano; Giorgio Ré, Ufficio Stampa Gianfranco Ferré, Milano; Giandomenico Romanelli, Civici Musei Veneziani d'Arte e di Storia, Venezia; Pierre Rosenberg, Musée du Louvre, Parigi; Cinzia Rosselli, Sartoria del Teatro alla Scala, Milano; Piera Rum, Ufficio Musei e Beni Culturali, Regione Liguria; Claudio Salsi, Civica Raccolta delle Stampe "A. Bertarelli", Milano; Bruno Santi, Sovrintendente per i Beni Artistici e Storici di Roma, Roma; Sandrino Schiffini, Civiche Raccolte Storiche, Milano; Sovrintendente dei Beni Artistici e Storici, Firenze; Claudio Strinati, Sovrintendente per i Beni Artistici e Storici di Roma, Roma; Andrea Tamoni, Archivio Fotografico del Teatro alla Scala, Milano; Tilde Tenconi, Milano; Maestro Gianpiero Tintori, Direttore Museo Teatrale alla Scala, Milano; Francesca Tosi, Ufficio Stampa Pucci, Firenze; Emanuela Tosti, Ufficio Stampa Capucci, Roma; Gabriele Valdata, Mandello del Lario; Gerolamo Valle, Impresa Mario Valle, Arenzano; Renzo Zorzi, Segretario Generale Fondazione Giorgio Cini, Venezia

Contents

THE REALM OF THE SENSES

Fabrizio de' Marinis

The most fanciful images of the weaver's art across the centuries: upon thrones, altars, in royal bed chambers, bourgeois drawing rooms and the ateliers of great couturiers; it is velvet which has marked entire eras. Like iron, fire, bronze, wool, and the silk of which it is the highest woven expression, velvet has accompanied the transformation of civilization throughout time in art and in daily life. From Byzantine courts to the Renaissance; from the Bauhaus to Cubism, its charm has hardly ever dwindled.

Velvet has clad kings and condottieri, saints and virgins, noblewomen and courtesans with its surreal dazzle. It has inspired great painters as they immortalized those figures who have made history age after age in their precious works.

The Church has long used velvet for important ceremonies and for the ceremonial garb of popes. Kings and emperors, wrapped in sumptuous velvets, have decreed wars and signed peace treaties, given birth to states and nations or signed their death warrants.

From the sumptuous apparel of Renaissance queens, to the less sumptuous outfits of Greta Garbo and Joan Crawford – less sumptuous, but still equally powerful in their hold on the imagination of women – velvet has established the rules and canons of elegance. And in theater as well it has held powerful sway. Giuseppe Verdi demanded only the finest velvet for the outfits of the characters in his operas, and the same was true of Rossini and Donizetti. From Caruso to Galeffi to Giuditta Pasta, one and all lavished maniacal attention to the velvety spectacle of the costumes of their operas. And what shall we say of the long list of designers, from Courrèges, Cardin, Rabanne, Marucelli, and De Barentzen?

Velvet, however, has been first and foremost an economic phenomenon, which has generated enormous wealth, enough to pay armies, create banks, and radically shift the array of international economies.

A powerful lever in the great trade of the Renaissance, velvet made the fortunes of the bankers and merchants of city-states such as Lucca, Florence, and the maritime republics of Genoa and Venice. For centuries, these cities dominated the textiles markets of the entire world, with their velvets, influencing the prices of raw materials, commercial treaties, fashions, technology, and new discoveries. Subsequently, with the advent of mechanized production on a grand scale, it was the French textile-manufacturing towns, and especially Lyon, that enjoyed the benefits of the huge rivers of cash that were generated by the manufacture and sale of velvet. It was no accident that Napoleon personally oversaw the rebirth of the textiles industry of Lyon, as in their time the Medici and the Sforza, the Este and the Gonzaga had done.

Historical phenomena of great breadth and scope, which united some peoples and cultures on the venerable Silk Road, and divided others, between the East and the West, have become intertwined with what for centuries was the cloth of kings, the emblem of prestige and wealth, synonymous with privilege, in sacred and profane iconography.

Noblewomen, princesses, sovereigns, knights, great merchants, condottieri, and ambassadors made immortal by the greatest painters of the Renaissance, all remind us from their perches in major art galleries how extensive the use of these lavish fabrics was. The most illustrious painters, from Giotto to Piero della Francesca and Raphael, gave almost the same importance to the velvets in the portraits they painted as to the faces.

Velvet, in other words, when woven with the most valued mater-

9

ials, such as gold and silver, was for a long time one of the most sophisticated and valuable products of the weaver's art. And in its history there is a touch of mystery. We are still ignorant of its origins, in fact.

The earliest traces of velvet are lost somewhere on the legendary Silk Road, the great transcontinental caravan route that connected Lo-Yang (the Sinae Metropolis mentioned by Ptolemy) with Ch'ang-an (Sera Metropolis) through the Taklamakan, the desert without return, all the way to the port cities of the eastern Mediterranean.

A great many peoples were brought into contact by trade in velvet: Orientals, Mediterraneans, Europeans. We can almost imagine those merchants, caravans, and travellers of distant times, wending their way slowly along sandy tracks and through the dusty marketplaces of cities like Samarkand. Many chronicles of bygone eras speak at length about them, discussing the trade treaties between city-states and maritime republics, the detailed notes of Flemish merchants and avid Londoners.

A great deal of history has occurred since then. But velvet, perhaps because of the magic of its soft and intriguing structure, as pleasing to the finger as to the eye, has continued to live and to adjust to new eras. And so from the oriental "Alambras", we find velvet on the throne of the Medici. We glimpse it in antique paintings, under the armor of Renaissance warriors such as Malatesta, Federico da Montefeltro, and Bartolomeo Colleoni. It surrounds nude women and coy cupids. And at the birth of every new school, such as Art Nouveau or Bauhaus, this fabric is once again brought to the forefront with determination by the "maîtres à penser", revised and redesigned.

Even the Beatles, in the Sixties, when they sang "Let It Be", in London for the first time, were wearing four close-fitting jackets in black velvet. And that's not all: just as in the carriages of princes and kings, so too the bench seats of Rolls Royces are upholstered in velvet, a special fabric developed by an Italian company, the Redaelli company of Mandello del Lario.

As to the origins of velvet, scholars from all over the world have discussed and debated for many years. It is now a general belief that this fabric, originally made of silk, arrived in Italy for the first time from the Far East, transported by Arab merchants, and was then spread throughout Europe, in turn, by merchants from Lucca, Venice, Florence, and Genoa.

In Italy, beginning in the twelfth century and continuing through the entire eighteenth century, the largest industry for the production of velvets in the western world was set up. For centuries Lucca, Siena, Venice, Florence and Genoa supplied the rest of Europe with these valued fabrics, to be used in clothing, wall coverings, upholstery, the trappings of horses, furniture of all sorts, and the interiors of carriages and litters.

The documents of the period provide ample descriptions of how immense wealth and huge fortunes were generated during the Renaissance by velvet merchants. Their guild was one of the most powerful in the entire Renaissance, and it overtopped the guilds of woolmakers and silkmakers during the fourteenth and fifteenth centuries. A considerable part of the vast fortunes of families such as the Medici, the Este, the Sforza and the Gonzaga had been taken from trade in velvet. And the banks of Florence, Venice, and Genoa already dominated international finance through a complex intertwining of letters of credit and futures contracts to fix prices of raw materials – silks and dyeing materials – in advance.

A great deal of debate over the origins of velvet has taken place.

On page 8:
Jean Auguste Dominique Ingres,
Napoleon Bonaparte, First Consul.
Musée d'Art Moderne, Liège.

Titian, *The Venus of Urbino.*
The Uffizi, Florence.

Titian, *Federico Gonzaga, Duke of Mantua.*
Palatine Gallery, Florence.

Titian, *Portrait, known as La Bella.*
Palatine Gallery, Florence.

Many historians claim that the earliest velvets were woven in Palermo, in imitation of the velvets from the east. The hypothesis that this precious cloth was first woven in Sicily and later spread to the rest of Italy was first put forth by the French scholar A. Latour.

Many other scholars tend to favor the Venetian route, since we have documentation from as early as the ninth to eleventh centuries of intense trade between Venice and the East. Strangely enough, however, in his accounts dating from 1189 on the ateliers of Palermo, entitled "Liber de Regno Siciliae", the Sicilian chronicler Ugo Falcando, though he does write extensively on the art of silk spinning and weaving in this city, makes no mention whatever of the weaving of velvet.

Arabic, at any rate, is the only language that makes use of the name of a city Kathifet in mentioning velvet. This city may well be the place where this type of cloth was produced for the first time. Here in Italy, on the other hand, the fabric takes its name from the characteristic appearance – in Italian, "vello" means fleece, and "velluto", or velvet, means fleecy. Scholars such as the Frenchman Bezon, and before him the authors of the Encyclopédie Méthodique, sustain that velvet was first woven in the Indies, while others, such as Algoud, do not even rule out a Chinese origin for the fabric.

Another author of the Encyclopédie, A. Latour, instead, claims that the fabric was first manufactured in Persia, based on archeological finds (thirteenth-fourteenth centuries) still preserved in the Musée Historique des Tissus, in Lyon. An origin, in other words, that still causes debate.

The splendors of city-states and republics, in a stupendous explosion of vitality, creativity, and art, put Italy at the head of the civilized world and made her a mistress of fashions, which she knew perfectly how to mingle with styles and luxury.

Isabella d'Este, Duchess of Milan, "inventor of fashions", obtained the assistance of the most illustrious artists – even Leonardo da Vinci – in designing and creating her clothing, and with a procession of ladies and cavaliers in ceremonial garb she succeeded in amazing even the reputedly splendid king of France, Charles VIII, in 1494. Catherine de' Medici (1519-1589), when she was married to King Henry II, brought to France all the spendor of Florentine elegance, largely made up of lavish outfits made of extremely fine velvets, a fabric in which Florence, during the sixteenth century, had attained uncontested leadership.

During the Renaissance, velvet acquired a vast importance in clothing, as in interior decoration. Due to its magnificence, the particularity of its three-dimensional nature, and the great variety of types and designs, it almost magically represented every aspect of the period. The textile structure of the cloth – which unlike other fabrics has a "third dimension" as well, the depth of the pile – and the complexity of its manufacture, make it practically an emblem of the investigative mindset of the Renaissance, which was to rifle through almost every aspect of existence during those years, from artistic standards to industrial methods.

Fabrics with piles had been manufactured ever since distant times. They could be woven on almost any home loom. Velvet, on the other hand, was made on extremely complex looms, which called for a level of crafstmanship and a refined and specialized tradition of weaving. In fact, even Leonardo da Vinci spent some time and energy studying these revolutionary tools.

One need only take a look at the ancient "Mariegole", the statutes of the guild of the "veluderi", or velvet weavers, of Venice, and of the weavers of Florence and Genoa, to realize just how complex the production of velvet actually was. In Venice, where in the sixteenth

Parmigianino, *Galeazzo Sanvitale*.
Museum of Capodimonte, Naples.

Dosso Dossi, *The Sorceress Circe*.
Borghese Gallery, Rome.

century there were over four thousand looms in operation, the "Corte da Paragon" ensured an extremely high level of professional standards. The "Corte" was an office that displayed and sold only textiles, after establishing the high quality of the raw materials employed and of the manufacturing process.

It was established that both simple and ornate velvets could have no fewer than three hundred threads per ligature and no fewer than eighteen ligatures (at least 5400 threads), and must have gold in the selvage, used to read the type dyes used.

No fabric in history has been studied and painted as often and as thoroughly as velvet. Certainly, it was much admired and sought after by the courts, due to its elegance, and by merchants, for its high margins of profitability, but it was even more sought after and admired by artists, for the unpredictable nature of its shades and nuances, produced by the way in which light hit it.

In fifteenth- and sixteenth-century Italy, for instance, artists such as Crivelli, Antonello da Messina, and Bartolomeo Vivarini studied velvet, analyzing its structure and the difficulties of reproducing its appearance, and full-fledged treatises were written on the subject. During the same period, elsewhere in Europe, painters such as Jan van Eyck and Hans Memling wrote treatises on the same subject. Even Michelangelo worked to design special types of velvet, destined to the sumptuous robes of kings and popes.

And the same phenomenon can be found in later periods: in Lyon, between the seventeenth and eighteenth centuries, with Revel, Watteau, and Berain; later on with Art Nouveau, Art Deco, the Bauhaus, and the flourishing of synthetic and artificial fibers. Mucha, Van de Velde, Mackintosh, and Mies van der Rohe all worked with the complex structure of velvet.

And the charm of velvet has continued to seduce, right up to modern times, influencing fashion and furnishings, from Florentine furniture of the Renaissance, up until the Fauves and Cubist art.

Sentiment is still aroused by the scenes of the hunt, symbolic scenes of springtime, rural dances, and scenes of work in the fields as found in the "decor naturaliste" of Fontainebleau, the Elysée, the Tuilleries, and Malmaison; the Victorian furnishings of English country homes and castles; the revolutionary design of the Bauhaus.

In the area of high fashion, Balmain, Valentino, Saint Laurent, and Capucci, have all consecrated, in our time, the seductive powers of velvet. And prêt-à-porter has also claimed velvet as its own, thanks to the work of a great many Italian and French manufacturers, such as Redaelli, Visconti di Modrone, Bianchini Ferrier, Chatillon, Ducharne, Hurrell, and Legler.

In close relation with what has happened in the world of art, velvet has always been the trigger of vast economic shifts. We mentioned this at the outset, referring to the republics of Genoa, "La Superba", and Venice, "La Serenissima". Velvet has exerted an influence that has affected every sector of technology, from research into new and revolutionary raw materials, to the looms, the methods of weaving, and the treatment of the fabric. The Lyonnais period and the splendors of Napoleon's time, above all, mark the entry of velvet into technological modernity, with the inventions of Claude Dangon and Joseph Marie Jacquard.

The "bottega" of the Renaissance was by this point only a vague memory. The masses of the nineteenth century and an advancing middle class were eager to possess what had once been the fabrics of royal splendor. The Age of Reason had unlocked increasingly new horizons.

And velvet was to follow, step by step, every shift and change,

Titian, *The Emperor Charles V at the Battle of Muhlberg.* Museo Nacional del Prado, Madrid.

Titian, *Proclamation of the Marquis of Vasto.* Museo Nacional del Prado, Madrid.

every new fashion, without ever losing its identity, adapting perfectly to the new technological transformations of the textile industry, changes which were to modify manufacturing equipment completely.

Quite quickly the looms of the past were nothing but a memory. The first efforts to weave double velvet mechanically date from the end of the eighteenth century. An old catalogue for the Exposition of Saint Etiènne, in France, mentioned a certain Monsieur Thiolliere David who, in 1793, for the first time, introduced a loom in his factory which could be used to weave double velvet. But we have no idea of who the inventor of this new technology might have been.

Patents for the production of velvet with this revolutionary technique were registered at the beginning of the nineteenth century, both in France and in England and the United States. The first patent was registered by a Frenchman, in 1808. It was a loom capable of weaving double strips of velvet, which were then cut by a sharp blade, which ran on a small track.

In 1824, Steven Wilson, an Englishman, patented a similar loom in London. In 1833, it was the turn of Jean Baptiste Martine, from Tarare, a town in the south of France, who perfected the system while making it still more rapid and efficient. In 1852, on the other hand, a certain Samuel Holt patented two new machines in England, which made it possible to weave double velvet, without the use of the devices invented by Jacquard, and to cut the two pieces with a mechanical system, replacing the former manual system. In 1878, Samuel Lister and Jose Reixach, both from Manningham, England, developed a modern system for cutting which received a patent in Great Britain during the same year, and then in 1879 in France and Germany and in 1884 in the United States.

Velvet had by this point entered the modern age. The growing demand of increasingly huge markets, starved for new developments, incremented exponentially the technological improvements required for producing ever increasing quantities, to the point that there sprang up, alongside the great textile groups, a myriad of specialized industrial companies which made the machinery and looms for the weaving of velvet.

In Lyon, the Beridot company was established, winning widespread fame, while in Krefeld, Germany, the Thonner and the Gusken companies were founded; in Belgium, the Van de Viele company was well known. And during this same period, other great inventions were developed, such as the loom with two opposing shuttles, for the weaving of double velvet, the forerunner of modern pincer looms, which definitively revolutionized the sector, beginning in 1865.

The Renaissance "bottega" of the guilds and the quality of the creations of that institution were now finally and completely relegated to the past. What had once been Italian strongholds of velvet were now defended as best seemed possible. For the entire middle portion of the nineteenth century, Italian production, save for creations of extremely high quality, continued to decline much as it had in the previous century. It was in 1860 that a first recovery began in Liguria, at Zoagli, with the processing of smooth velvets. In 1866, the duke Visconti di Modrone founded the first corduroy factory.

In 1893, Alfredo Redaelli founded in Rancio, not far from Lecco in Northern Italy, the first Italian weaving mill for double velvet, both for clothing and for interior decoration. This enterprising industrialist, after spending many years in Krefeld, Germany, specialized in the new technologies developed by the Germans and then returned to Italy, developing his own fabrics mill, soon earning a great international reputation, and receiving huge orders from France, Germany, England, and even the Far East.

But this is already the history of modern velvet, which has witnessed the proliferation of great manufacturing centers not only in Italy (the manufacturing centers of Brianza are particularly well known for the jacquard fabrics for interior decoration), but also in France, Germany, Belgium, and England, and above all in the United States, where much of the resources and energy of Europe found their way, with specialists who established themselves in Connecticut, New Jersey, Pennsylvania, and New York.

Of particular historical stature is the name of Gertrude Rapp, the true founder of this textile art in the New World, in 1840.

After 1880, in the meanwhile, a few courageous craftsmen had rediscovered, in Italy, the practice of figured velvets, especially for the furnishing industry (velluti di ordito, or warp pile velvet), and they remain even today the most refined in the world. In Venice, Luigi Bevilacqua (1882) and L. Rubelli, who succeeded in 1892 to G.B. Trapolin, in Milan Vittorio Ferrari (1891), in Florence Lisio (1906). The latter, a close friend of the poet Gabriele D'Annunzio, manufactured a number of velvets and damasks for the Vittoriale, D'Annunzio's villa. He was responsible for the rediscovery of many of the decorative motifs taken directly from the paintings by masters of the Renaissance, and among those paintings was Botticelli's *Primavera*. The history of this fabric, which was the cloth of kings and queens, noblewomen and knights, in other words, has enjoyed a surprising degree of continuity. It has proceeded apace with the changes in customs and markets, adapting to new situations with consummate skill. From a rich symbol of power, as it was in the Renaissance, it was transformed into an emblem of refinement for the vast middle classes in modern Europe, and then with high fashion it revived the splendors of other times. And with the prêt-à-porter industry, lastly, it was delivered to a larger public, once again facing the challenge, with surprising transformations, of the styles, trends, and innovations of our modern days.

Jean Auguste Dominique Ingres,
Napoleon upon the Imperial Throne.
Musée de l'Armée, Paris.

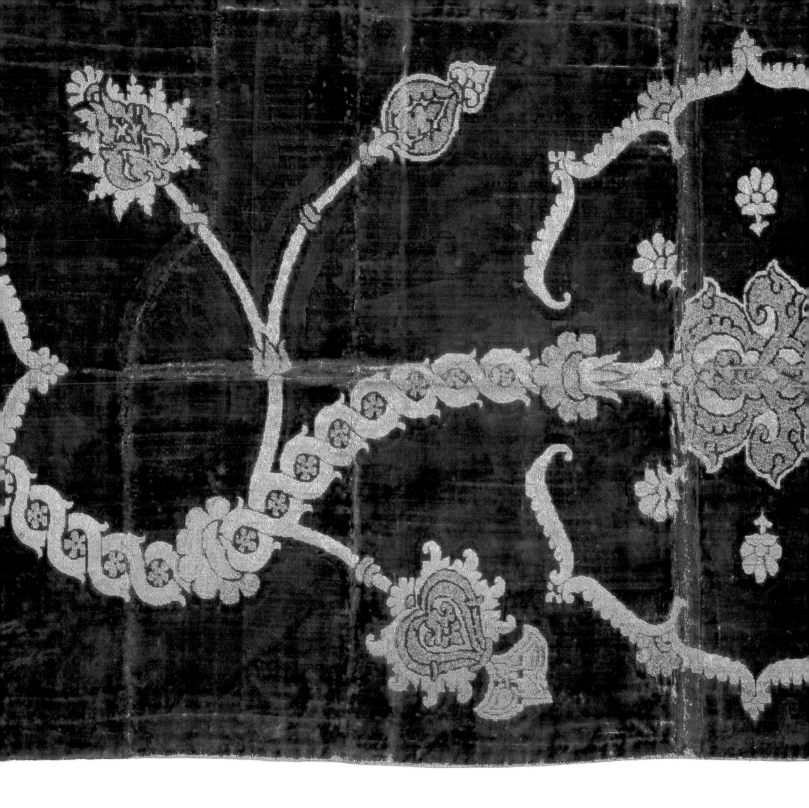

Silk pile on pile velvet with gold brocading wefts.
Venice (?), second half of the fifteenth century.
The Metropolitan Museum of Art, New York.

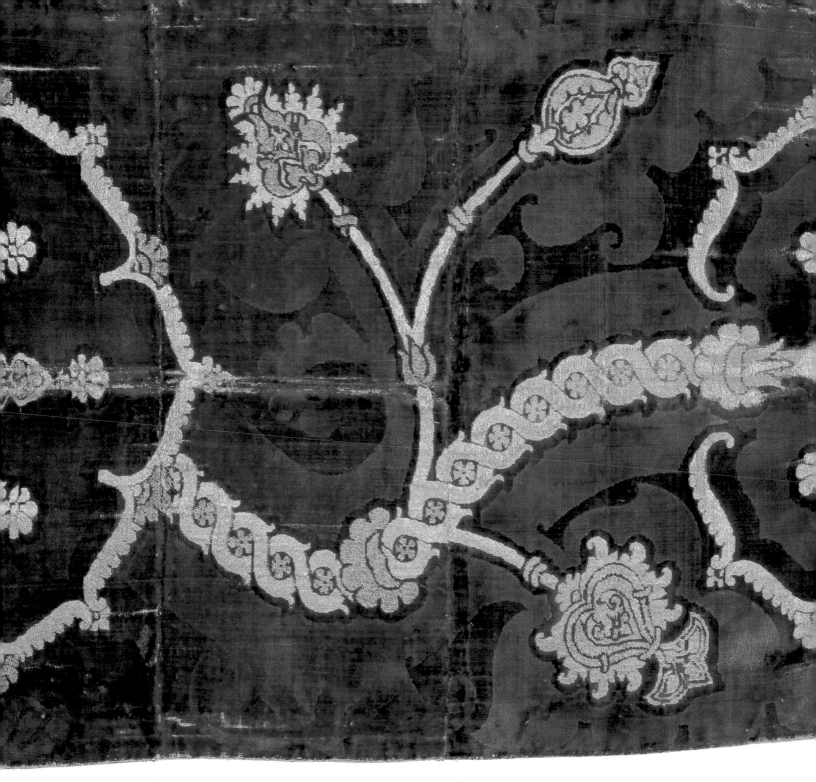

THE TRIUMPH OF VELVET
Italian production of velvet
in the Renaissance

Roberta Orsi Landini

Velvet established itself as the king of fabrics in the fifteenth century. In the theater of appearances and in the codification of social hierarchies, where clothing has always played an extremely significant role, the presence of velvet indicated the nobility and importance of the personages that wore it. In the frescoes, tapestries, paintings, and miniatures that preserve the splendor of the courts and the solemnity of religious ceremonies, the same silken velvets, glittering with wefts of gold, adorn, surround, and identify the saints, the powerful, and the kings. If the union of these two precious materials had already been known and reserved for many centuries to the highest social classes, the form in which they were produced in the fifteenth century – that of velvet brocaded with gold – was relatively new and remarkable in its effects and in the techniques of its production.

Neither the sumptuous Byzantine and Persian silk samites, nor the lampas of the fourteenth century, with their incredible designs, the pride of the manufacturers of Lucca, offered the remarkable array of esthetic possibilities of velvet. Moreover, they could not embody so solidly and visibly the idea that the person wearing it was aware of living in a new era: in the fifteenth century, especially in Italy, the center of velvet production, power no longer signified birth and descent, but rather – and above all – money and wealth.

What was considered the overriding feature of silk yarn, in the Chinese tradition and in the West during the Middle Ages, was its remarkable fineness, which allowed the weaving of cloth with a lightness and a sheen that could not be equalled. Silk clothing, worn by emperors, popes, and kings, suggested an image of otherworldly lightness. Silk enveloped those who wore it in shiny soft drapery, which at once covered and revealed, as was appropriate to those who were manifestations of divinity.

In comparison with the silks of Byzantium, Persia, and Lucca, velvet appeared as a heavy, solid, substantial fabric; the limbs that were covered by velvet did not appear to be transfigured, but rather redesigned in plastic terms. At its first appearance, velvet proved to be a fabric of unquestionable manly connotations, the perfect ornament of princes and condottieri.

The possession of velvet was a sign of power and wealth, but at the same time it created wealth and power for those who knew the secrets of making it. With the sumptuary laws that established and limited the uses to which it could be put, velvet became the symbol of rigid social hierarchies, while in its actual use it subverted order and values. Accessible to a growing number of people, velvet came to acquire over the course of the fifteenth century an increasing range of distinctive marks, which underscored its price, rareness, and importance, in a vain effort to establish itself as an exclusive and elite product.

The most ancient velvets that we still possess, which date from the fourteenth century, are fewer in number, but no less interesting for that [1]. Aside from a few fairly simple striped or finely checkered fragments, a number of important pieces bear out the indications we have obtained from written sources of the epoch, according to which, over the course of the century, and especially in the last quarter century, there was a growing presence of figured and polychrome velvets, some brocaded with gold, in the royal wardrobes. The value of these velvets was far superior to that of all other fabrics, especially when they were dyed in the prized chermes red. These acquired the lead in luxury textiles produced for the powerful in just a few years, displacing samite, which had formerly dominated the world of silk textiles uncontested.

Purse made of silk velvet with gold brocading wefts.
Italy, second half of the fourteenth century.
Pinacoteca Comunale, Spoleto.

Derek Bouts the Younger, *The Justice of Otto. Ordeal by Fire.* 1470-1475.
Musées Royaux des Beaux-Arts de Belgique, Brussels.

21

Silk cut voided velvet
with gold brocading
and bouclé wefts.
Florence, third quarter
of the fifteenth century.
Musée Historique des
Tissus, Lyon.

Silk cut voided velvet
with gold brocading
wefts.
Venice, first half of the
fifteenth century.
Musée Historique des
Tissus, Lyon.

On page 24:
Silk solid cut velvet
with three pile warps of
different colours.
Italy, end of the
fourteenth century.
Musée Historique des
Tissus, Lyon.

On page 25:
Silk cut voided two pile
warps velvet, with the
heraldic device of the
Soderini family.
Florence, second half of
the fifteenth century.
Musée Historique des
Tissus, Lyon.

Production and processing

It is quite likely that the town of Lucca was responsible for introducing velvet to the markets of Europe. Lucca's reputation as the leading manufacturing center in the west in the fourteenth century was bound with the technical quality and the decorative imagination found in its samites and lampas, often with brocading gold wefts. The examples of this magnificent production that have survived to the modern day are eloquent of a truly revolutionary inventiveness in the designs, with respect to the repetitive and static formulas found in the ornamental structure of Byzantine and Muslim silks. The motifs showed the influence of a broad array of different cultures, deriving from the Arab, Chinese, and Persian worlds. In these designs there was movement, and not the static vision that appeared in earlier versions. On the silks of Lucca, animals run, fly, chase each other, shaking their tails, paws, and manes; the forms of the plants twist and flex in sinuous movements; streams gush forth and rays of sunlight dart swiftly. Through a nature that is depicted in a constant state of transformation, the new style manifested by this type of textile decoration clearly revealed the sentiments and awareness of a society that had undergone change and was continuing to change, of new social classes that were acquiring power and creating new political institutions.

Craftsmen and merchants were organizing themselves into guilds, capable not only monitoring the behavior of their members and the quality of the products that those members were manufacturing and selling in far-off lands, but also of leading and governing cities. In this période, the production of silk was no longer – and had not been for some time – the privilege of imperial ateliers, like those in Palermo and Byzantium, where there was a strict control over the types of silk produced and their final destinations. The possibility of producing silk more freely must have constituted in cities such as Lucca – where the finest craftsmen in the trade worked – a powerful stimulus not only for experimentation in graphic terms, but also in terms of technique; these impulses grew as the demand became more various with the spread of the trade routes and the improvement of quality of life in the west[2]. The actual invention of velvet is still a historical mystery[3]. Its origins should be sought out in the workshops that specialized in the production and processing of silk, where the luminous qualities of silk were exalted to the greatest possible degree by special weaving techniques. By the time it appeared on western markets and received mention in documents, velvet was already a luxury product, the result of a process in which generations of specialized weavers perfected the loom, its shape, the various devices, the size, and the way of building the tools needed for the formation of the pile, and found the optimal weave, the best arrangement of the threads in the warps, the correct degrees of tension.

The earliest documents that testify not only to the production of velvet in Lucca, Venice, Florence, and Genoa, but also to the presence of velvet in royal and papal inventories, date from the beginning of the fourteenth century[4]. As a fabric worthy of being worn by the highest authorities, the qualities of velvet must already have been supported, at the dawn of the fourteenth century, by consolidated standards of production, which made velvet a product with constant and reliable esthetic and technical features.

The first codification of the rules of manufacturing velvet that we know about appears in the Statute of the Court of the Merchants of Lucca, dated 1376[5]. These rules give us an idea of the variety and the elevated level of the types of velvet being produced then, and it

clearly attests to the conclusion of a lengthy and laborious process in developing the procedures for weaving the fabric, and the machinery with which to weave it. The most valued type was velvet with brocading gold wefts, the production of which required enormous specialization within the ranks of the already greatly specialized weavers of velvet. No less remarkable were the polychrome velvets, obtained through the use of double, triple, and at times even quadruple warps of pile, especially those on a white background, the weaving of which involved some very delicate work. Then came velvets with different heights of pile, which gave the fabric the appearance of a bas-relief. Last were the figured velvets on satin ground and the simple, but no less superb, solid velvets.

It is thus not surprising that velvet weavers, or "vellutai", already had by the middle of the fourteenth century, in Genoa and Venice, separate guilds or associations within the ranks of the weavers at large[6]. Their technical knowledge could only be deduced in part – that is to say, reconstructed by an expert colleague – from their

creations. The tools needed to form the pile of velvet and the methods of weaving were not easily determined by analyzing the fabric itself, and therefore constituted trade secrets that it was wise to conceal jealously. If there were only a relatively few centers of manufacture, there were even fewer weavers in those centers capable of producing the handsomest and most prestigious pieces of work. Their skill and their knowledge constituted a considerable economic resource for the community. No specialized craftsman was allowed to leave the city without permission; going to work in rival cities was equivalent to an automatic confiscation of all one owned and a certain death sentence.

The esthetic qualities of this new type of fabric so greatly increased the demand in the various courts of Europe that, from the end of the fourteenth century onward, other important weaving cities aside from Lucca, such as Florence, Venice, and Genoa, began to specialize in the production of velvet. In western silk manufacture, it was these latter who rivaled each other, in the fifteenth and

sixteenth century, for leadership in luxury textile manufacturing; and it was they who gave a modern aspect to the entrepreneurial activity involved, supplying a financial and commercial organization of international breadth.

While the acquisition of velvets brocaded with gold wefts required extremely significant amounts of money – it was no accident that the outfits themselves, or portions of them, such as the sleeves, made of this fabric appeared in the official lists of items in dowries[7] – vast amounts of capital were required to finance their manufacture. The cost of the raw materials for the most handsome dyes, almost all of which had to be imported from elsewhere, was very high[8]. Aside from the silk, which is used in velvet in amounts three times greater than what is required in other types of fabrics, it was the silver and gold so often used in the manufacture that drove up the costs involved, to the degree and the manner in which those substances were used. Goldsmiths were also members of the Silk Manufacturers' Guild, and among them were a number of extremely skilled specialists, such as the "battilori" and the "tiralori", i.e., the "gold pounders" and the "gold pullers", who worked to create the extremely fine yarns that could be used in weaving. In order to produce a valuable fabric, especially a velvet, the work of a vast number of artisans was required, from the humble spinners, to the most highly specialized master craftsmen. Silk was the foundation upon which a great portion of the economy of leading manufacturing towns was based, because the majority of the population labored over it on a daily basis. The weaving of the most lavish fabrics took place only inside the city walls, where the entire process could be meticulously controlled in each of the various phases – each piece of silk fabric, in fact, had to be checked and marked in order to be suitable for sale on foreign markets – and in the physical presence of the master craftsmen, who possessed knowledge and lore that was crucial to the prosperity of the city.

And so this was clearly a type of manufacturing that could prosper only if there were huge amounts of capital available to fund it: the best known bankers of Florence, including the Medici, invested in the production of precious silks, and then sold those silks through the various market towns which were the headquarters of their leading financial agents, such as Bruges, Geneva, and Lyon. The quality of the cloth that they manufactured appears to be described analytically in the family portrait limned by the brush of Benozzo Gozzoli on the walls of the chapel in the Medici family palazzo, in the fairy tale narration of the cavalcade of the Three Magi[9]. Cosimo the Elder is shown dressed in a sober but extremely refined black pile-on-pile velvet; black and gold and crimson and gold was worn by his son Piero; the Magi and all of the personages in the procession display a very lavish ranges of fabrics, which was certainly representative of those produced by the family and by the city of Florence; among those fabrics, there was a prevalence of green, red, and white – either together or separately – which were the colors of the Medici uniforms. Studies made of the accounting books of a number of Florentine companies, such as the book of the workshop of the silk manufacturer Andrea Banchi in the fifteenth century[10], and that of the Strozzi and Capponi families in the sixteenth century[11], provide a variety of useful information that helps us to understand the actual monetary worth of velvets containing gold and silk, which became a symbol of royalty for excellent reasons. The salaries of the velvet weavers – if we leave aside the weavers of solid velvets – far outdistanced those of their colleagues specializing in other types of fabric, and they increased in direct proportion to the degree of difficulty of the work involved. At the

Benozzo Gozzoli, *Procession of the Three Magi*
(The Emperor John VIII Paleologus and entourage, with Cosimo the Elder).
1459-1462. Chapel in Palazzo Medici Riccardi, Florence.

Silk cut voided velvet with three pile warps and gold
brocading wefts, with the heraldic device of the Medici family.
Florence, last quarter of the fifteenth century.
Museo del Tessuto, Prato.

On page 26:
Silk cut voided velvet with three pile warps and gold brocading wefts.
Florence, last quarter of the fifteenth century.
Museo Nazionale del Bargello, Florence.

Agnolo Bronzino, *Eleonora of Toledo with her son John*, ca. 1445.
The Uffizi, Florence.

Silk cut voided velvet with brocading and bouclé wefts in gold and silver.
(*"riccio sopra riccio"* velvet).
Florence, second quarter of the sixteenth century.
Museo Civico di Torino, Turin.

bottom of the wage scales were the weavers of solid velvets; at the top of the scale, and well ahead of any and all competition, there were the weavers of pile-on-pile velvets with brocading and "bouclé" gold wefts. These craftsmen earned at least three times what the lowliest velvet weavers made, and they produced less than half the quantity of velvet than the others. In the middle, in increasing order in terms of salaries, were the weavers of pile-on-pile velvets, of polychrome velvets, and brocaded velvets[12].

The amount of time required for the production of pile-on-pile velvets brocaded with gold yarns, much sought after by foreign courts, was quite extensive, and only a few centimeters of the fabric could be produced each day. When the weaver was not forced to stop production due to illness or other unforeseen eventualities, he could not produce much more than 100 braccia, or just about 200 feet, in a year[13]. There were relatively few of these craftsmen in Florence, which was one of the finest manufacturers; according to the records of Andrea Banchi, who produced only high-quality cloth, there was only one weaver of pile-on-pile velvets brocaded with gold, out of the twenty-nine weavers in his employ. If Banchi could rely on only one master craftsmen to make gold and silver velvets, then the other eighty leading silk manufacturers in the city[14] could not have been employing many more. In the following century, Eleonora of Toledo, the wife of Cosimo I de' Medici, who was particularly fond of fine cloth, had two of these master craftsmen at her service – remarkably, one of these was a woman – working in Palazzo Vecchio. These two craftsmen were probably the weavers of the magnificent "arabesqued" velvet with gold and silver weft loops that Eleonora wears in the portrait that Agnolo Bronzino painted of her[15].

The silk manufacturer almost always sold products that had already been produced; quite often, however, he was asked to produce to order, which meant executing specific design, generally containing heraldic crests. The already astronomical costs of production thus grew even more greatly, with the expenses of the new design and its programming on the loom. In some such cases, it became necessary to build special looms, far broader than the average loom; these looms required three, rather than the more standard two persons to operate them. Generally speaking, the standard width in the production of a hand-woven silks was no more than 54-60 centimeters; if the cloth became any wider, then serious difficulties arose in production. In the case of velvets, in particular, this width was obligatory in practical terms, so that it would be possible to insert the rods that raised the threads of the pile warp, of a length corresponding to the width of the fabric. The length of a human arm was the greatest distance allowed in the actual act of insertion of the rod, if this process was to remain reasonably efficient, so as not to hinder production. The designs produced in correspondence with the shape of the article to be manufactured (copes, altar-frontals) not only required a loom built to order, in which every article was made specifically to the desired width, but also rods manufactured specifically for the occasion. In order to insert longer rods, the weaver had to resort on these occasions to an assistant, who inserted and removed the rods at his command. The surviving examples of this type of production should certainly be considered among the finest masterpieces of the weaver's art. Particularly noteworthy is the altar-frontal of Assisi, bearing the crest of Sixtus IV della Rovere, woven to a width of 82-83 centimeters; even more extraordinary is the drape ordered by the English king Henry VII in the last year of the fifteenth century, in which the cloth attains a width of 140 centimeters. Velvets were

designed according to the objects that were to be made with them: in the case of copes or pluvials, in the shape of a huge semicircle, where the heraldic emblems were arranged in such a way as to be displayed correctly once the cope was worn by the priest[16].

Florence, which was the site of production of these remarkable pieces of work, also boasted craftsmen who were remarkably skillful in the creation of brocade effects, which were particularly complex in the case of velvets. A typically Florentine specialty was the "riccio sopra riccio", which involved raising parts of the design with weft loops, one close to the next, often produced with brocaded silver and gold "filé" threads of differing dimensions. In this manner, it was possible to create a variety of light effects and levels of surface, which were added to the levels formed by the silk pile of the velvet.

The golden loop was obtained through wefts, and not with warp, as was the case with the pile of velvet. It is already found in the

descriptions of drapes found in royal inventories at the end of the fourteenth century[17], and was used to produce the effects of "allucciolato", i.e., sparkle effects scattered across the dark surface of the velvet area. By the end of fifteenth century, this technique was being used in increasingly ample surface areas, and in a few superb articles, those areas were larger than the areas in silk. The excellent quality of the design and the spectacular metal threads of the fabrics produced in Florence – such as the cope of Vallombrosa with Medici heraldic devices, the Passerini cope of Cortona, the cope with the heraldic devices of Leon and Castille, donated by Queen Isabella to the first bishop of Granada – made them, despite the remarkable quantity of gold used in them, extremely flexible and yielding fabrics, an expression of great wealth and, at the same time, of incomparable elegance.

Cope in cut voided velvet with gold brocading and bouclé wefts, donated by Isabela of Castile to the first bishop of Granada. ("*riccio sopra riccio*" velvet).
Florence, end of the fifteenth century.
Musée Historique des Tissues, Lyon.

On page 30:
Cope of the Passerini vestments, in cut voided velvet with gold brocading and bouclé wefts. ("*riccio sopra riccio*" velvet).
Florence, first decade of the sixteenth century.
Church of Saint Francis, Cortona.

Maestro dell'Osservanza, *Nativity of Mary*, ca. 1450.
Museo d'Arte Sacra, Asciano.

Silk cut pile on pile velvet.
Italy, first quarter of the fifteenth century.
Museo Civico di Torino, Turin.

The motifs

Fifteenth-century production of velvets was marked by two very distinct designs, one of which was a sinuous and wide pattern unit, the other being a symmetrical modular structure. The fundamental pattern of both these designs was the so-called pomegranate motif, enclosed in great lobed petals. Textiles designers continued to use this pattern in endless variations in the two different structural solutions, which textiles historians, following an Italian source of the fifteenth century, have called, in the first case, "a griccia", (straight comber unit) and in the second, "a cammino" (reverse comber unit) [18].

There are a number of reasons for the repetition of the same design for more than a century, a phenomenon that appears exceedingly odd to our modern eyes, especially if we place it in the context of the remarkable proliferation of ideas and the dynamic explosion of painterly creativity that marked the fabrics of the fourteenth century. These reasons should be sought first and foremost in the significance of the pomegranate motif, which was a symbol of eternity, fertility, and resurrection, making it appropriate both for fabrics used by royalty and for sacred articles for the church; in the progressive development of new political institutions and in the philosophical definition of new esthetic ideas, with an ensuing

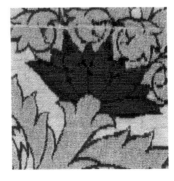

Jan van Eyck, *Madonna of the Chancellor Rolin*, ca. 1427. Musée du Louvre, Paris.

Detail of the workmanship of an altar frontal in ciselé pile on pile velvet with gold brocading and bouclé wefts. Genoa, end of the fifteenth century-beginning of the sixteenth century. Cathedral of San Lorenzo, Genoa.

On page 35:
Silk cut voided velvet with gold brocading and bouclé wefts.
Florence, 1470-1480.
Civici Musei Veneziani d'Arte e di Storia.
Cini Collection, Venice.

codification of formal values within the various states that manufactured the fabrics in question; in the slow process of manufacturing these fabrics and in the enormous related expense of modifying the patterns, especially if they were ample in size; and above all in the incredibly lavish nature of the most handsome articles which made the pomegranate the emblem of a certain status and the most eloquent medium for the ostentation of that status.

The so-called design "a griccia" clearly derived from the lively and sinuous patterns of the late fourteenth century. Produced in velvet for all the fifteenth century, it attained a definitive and monumental version in the earliest years of the century, which was

Hans Memling, *Mystical Marriage of Saint Catherine*, 1479.
Hans Memlingmuseum, Bruges.

Silk cut pile on pile velvet with gold brocading and bouclé wefts.
Florence, last quarter of the fifteenth century.
Poldi Pezzoli Museum, Milan.

to make it – when enriched with wefts of gold – in absolute terms the most valued and costly of fabrics. The asymmetrical structure of the motif, which unfolded across the entire width of the fabric, attaining vertical dimensions of over a meter, was in itself a valued feature, which made the articles considerably more difficult to produce, justifying a proportional increase in price.

In the earliest documentation available concerning this type of decoration manufactured with a golden ground, the figured part, which was often pile-on-pile velvet, constituted the focal point of the composition. As the century went on, the golden ground began to take on predominant importance; the areas of velvet pile tended

Carlo Crivelli, *Saint George* (detail of polytych), 1473.
Cathedral, Ascoli Piceno.

Silk cut voided velvet.
Florence, second quarter of the fifteenth century.
Museo Nazionale del Bargello, Florence.

Dalmatic in cut voided velvet, with embroidered appliqués.
Italy, middle of the fifteenth century.
Musée Historique des Tissus, Lyon.

Chasuble in cut voided velvet with orphrey in lampas.
Florence, third quarter of the fifteenth century.
Pinacoteca Comunale, Todi.

Altar frontal (detail) in cut pile on pile velvet with gold brocading and bouclé wefts.
Florence, first decade of the sixteenth century.
Pinacoteca Comunale, Spoleto.

Silk cut pile on pile velvet with brocading and bouclé wefts.
Venice (?), first half of the sixteenth century.
Civici Musei Veneziani d'Arte e di Storia.
Cini Collection, Venice.

Silk ciselé velvet.
Genoa, second half of the sixteenth century.
Musée Historique des Tissus, Lyon.

Altar frontal (detail) in cut pile on pile velvet with gold brocading and bouclé wefts.
Venice (?), second half of the sixteenth century.
Civici Musei Veneziani d'Arte e di Storia.
Cini Collection, Venice.

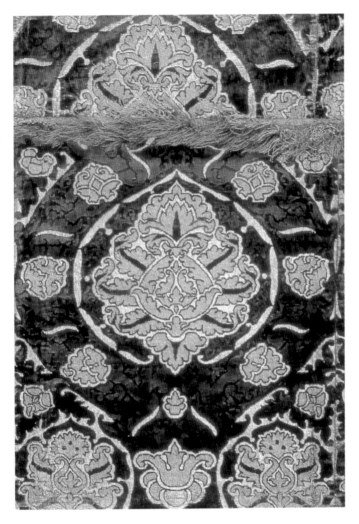

Silk cut pile-on-pile velvet, used by Venetian senators.
Venice, first half of the sixteenth century.
Musée Historique des Tissus, Lyon.

Giovan Battista Moroni, *Portrait of a Gentleman*, ca. 1540
Museo Nacional del Prado, Madrid.

to diminish until it was little more than a graphic sign, marking off the glittering areas of precious metal, in a design that was so articulated and complex that it became difficult to comprehend it as a whole, once the fabric took on the form of a finished object. Because of their unequalled economic and symbolic worth, these drapes were used as often in the manufacture or adornment – when employed in small quantities – of all sorts of apparel, overwear, and accessories; as ornamental covers of thrones and ceremonial chairs; as canopies in the pomp of ecclesiastical and secular ceremonies; and as sacred paraments of inestimable value. They represented the "prestige product" for the leading manufacturing towns in Italy, and they were much sought after in Italian and foreign courts; they were depicted and immortalized in portraits of kings and potentates.

Unlike the motif "a griccia", the design "a cammino", smaller in size and involving a more modest use of gold surfaces, presented around the middle of the century graphic designs and weaving techniques that were less massive and sumptuous. It was preferred for the production of the more simple "zetani vellutati", that is, figured velvet with satin ground weave, but the pattern was also used in the magnificent polychrome velvets. Its compositional equilibrium, more in tune with the standards of the Renaissance, made it the fabric of preference for the personal apparel of the more refined Florentines, such as the Medici, who relied upon culture, the promotion of the arts, and the development of a new esthetics to display their actual worldly power. The quality of design that is found in the lavish fabrics that bore their emblems – balls, plumes, rings with diamonds – invites us to subscribe to the seductive hypothesis that the leading painters, who worked to the greater glory of these princes, may also have supplied designs for some of the finer fabrics that they used or produced.

The fifteenth-century formula of the design "a cammino" – a pomegranate or a thistle flower, surrounded by small inflorescences – was to enjoy growing success and popularity from the middle of the century onward. It was to constitute the fundamental motif of textile decoration in the sixteenth century and, when fashion was to require new decorative patterns in fabrics used for clothing, it nonetheless continued to survive, practically until the present day, as a typical ornamental structure in fabrics for interior decoration.

Uses and fashions

In response to the demand for increasingly lavish velvet and gold fabrics, the manufacturing towns and centers responded with experimentation and the invention of new esthetic and technical effects that served to increase the worth of the fabric: enormous figures; increasingly extensive brocaded areas with gold "bouclé" wefts, of weft looped weave; the simultaneous presence of different heights of pile; the simultaneous presence of uncut and cut pile, or with all of these effects used at the same time.

The desire, however, to show off the leisure and wealth that they enjoyed drove the wealthy and powerful, and all those who wished to imitate their clothing and customs, not only to a mad competition in the purchase of increasingly expensive cloth of all sorts, but also to an excessive, pompous, and improper use of the same. From the simple display of wealth, they plummeted into an open and lavish wastage of resources: growing size of outfits, trains, sleeves dragging on the ground, linings more valuable than the outfits themselves, and lastly cuts on the fabric and lines that mutilated the design and forced the tailor to use increasingly vast quantities of

material. While men's and women's wardrobes grew and diversified into an ever greater number and variety of items of clothing, the outfits increasingly featured forms that hindered movement, accentuating all those features that had nothing to do with manual labor, such as the excessive length and volume of the gowns and exaggeratedly long and ample sleeves.

In claiming for itself the right to establish the operation of all of the systems of social distinction, the ruling class forced the governing authorities to issue an unending series of sumptuary laws, which reserved to the ruling class alone the consumption and use of precious materials and lavish fashions[19]. In all countries and states,

Petrus Christus, *Saint Eligio in His Goldsmithy*, 1449.
The Metropolitan Museum of Art, Robert Lehman Collection, New York.

both in Italy and elsewhere in the world, these decrees — which began to be issued during the thirteenth century — came one after the other at an increasing pace. The first sumptuary laws were meant to limit the excessive use of jewels and furs; velvet, which came closest to resembling fur in its appearance and feel and which made the greatest use of silk — a fiber that was by tradition reserved for the aristocratic classes — was generally forbidden or else permitted for only limited use, especially in its most lavish version, which is described by the legislators quite simply as "drappo d'oro", or golden cloth. Reckless spending on one's wardrobe, which was defined in the legislation, and quite wrongly, as a crime typical of

Setting Out for the Falcon Hunt.
Tapestry, Tournai (?), beginning of the sixteenth century.
Musée de Cluny, Paris.

Piero della Francesca, *Flagellation* (detail), ca. 1455.
Museo Civico di Palazzo Ducale, Urbino.

women[20], was indicated by the magistrates as the cause of ruin for both families and nations. Nonetheless, the wanton display of one's own economic power through the clothes one wore was allowed, in general, among young unmarried women, and for others on special occasions of private life (at weddings, for example) and, especially, of public life, when guests of great importance were being officially received in a city. The display of wealth through the luxury of one's wardrobe, then, was transformed from a private sin to a public duty with political goals. The lavish pomp of the courts, the grandiosity of appearances – where valued fabrics have always played a major role – have always been prime methods for the stimulation of admiration and, consequently, have been used to establish respect and to intimidate. Even in battle, this rule applied, and so great captains of armies, their steeds, their insignia, and the various apparatus were all clothed or draped in the greatest luxury and splendor. Thus sumptuary laws – which in any case never applied to sovereigns and aristocrats, whose life style was meant to bear witness at all times to the grandeur of the state – were enacted at ever increasing rates in the fifteenth and especially in the sixteenth centuries. While in the fifteenth century these laws tended to focus on the quality and quantity of valuable materials, in the following century, as an indicator of greater and more widespread wealth, these laws were more lenient concerning the use of valued fabrics, and tended to concentrate primarily on the fashions that promoted ostentation in the use of those fabrics.

The greatest and most lavish use of luxurious fabrics in the fifteenth century was through the fashion of tailoring in sloping pieces which, with the insertion of a number of triangles of fabric at approximately the height of the breast, made it possible to have very ample quantities of cloth at the bottom of the garment[21]. The design of figured fabrics (which constituted, according to the dimensions in question, or the weaving technique, one of the leading factors in the cost of the fabric) was thus mutilated and apparently eliminated as a valuable feature. This sort of apparel manufacture required, moreover, the purchase of increasingly abundant lengths of valuable fabrics, of which vast portions seemed to be destined for the scrap heap. In reality, of course, everything was carefully saved and reused in making shoes, purses, muffs, and borders; velvets with gold ground, which are particularly strong structurally, were used right down to the smallest snippets, and were always saved from discarded clothing, and recycled in other items. In the sixteenth century, the best way to display one's scorn for the richness of materials was that of dotting one's clothing with slits and slashes, in line with a fashion that was to last for more than a century. Generally, slashes were made in plain fabrics, satins, taffetas, and solid velvets, as a motif that became the chief decorative factor of the fabric, and at times of the outfit itself, ranging from the simplest to the most refined. When the fabric was cut, it was weakened, triggering a more rapid deterioration and, consequently, the need to replace it sooner. It was also less likely that the fabric could be reused in the manufacture of other objects or accessories. This practice, therefore, came within the sights of legislators, who limited or forbade its use.

Sumptuary laws were passed concerned the lavish pomp displayed not only through clothing, but also within the walls of the home: excessively lavish fabrics were forbidden even in canopies, blankets, curtains, and pillows. Despite the prohibitions, in the sixteenth century the use of valuable fabrics in the interiors of palaces and the homes of the wealthy became much more common and widespread; plain velvet, which served as a perfect substrate for embroideries in gold thread, appeared much more frequently, used to cover tables and to upholster and soften benches and stools.

For home furnishings and for clothing, on the other hand, until the middle of the century, the quality of velvets remained unaltered. Fashion then exalted solid and massive shapes, which were perfectly suited for shaping by the ample and rotund folds of velvet. In clothing, black became the century's favorite color, and silk and velvet surfaces gave the color an incredible sheen. Among black fabrics, velvet was unquestionably the most seductive one, with its shimmering surface ranging from deep shades to bright tints. The dyeing of velvet became a particular and unrivalled specialty of the leading manufacturing centers, such as Genoa, Florence, and Venice[22]. Even when Italian silk manufacturing lost its predominance in Europe, the black velvets being produced by these three Italian cities continued to be a source of pride and an important component of their exports.

Notes

[1]. On the earliest surviving examples of velvets, see L. Monnas, *Developments in Figured Velvet Weaving in Italy During the 14th Century*, in *Bulletin de Liaison du Centre International d'Etude des Textiles Anciens*, no. 63-64, I-II, 1986, pgg. 63-100.

[2]. Concerning manufacturing in Lucca, see D. Devoti, La seta. *Tesori di un'antica arte lucchese*. Lucca, 1989, with accompanying bibliography.

[3]. A brief history of velvet and its fundamental categories can be found in E. Bazzani, *Velluti di Seta*, in D. Devoti-G. Romano (edited by), *Tessuti antichi nelle chiese di Arona*, Turin, 1981, with accompanying bibliography.

[4]. L. Monnas, *Silk Cloths Purchased for the Great Wardrobe of the Kings of England*, in *Textile History*, vol. 20, no. 2, 1989, pgg. 283-320 for the English court; D. Devoti, op. cit., 1989 for the papal court; and for France, Douet d'Arcq, *Comptes de l'Argenterie des Rois de France au XIVe Siècle*, Paris, 1851; A.A.V.V., *Le Vêtement 1851: Histoire, archéologie, et symbolique, Vestimentaires au Moyen Age*, Paris, 1989, and F. Piponnier, *Emplois et diffusion de la soie en France à la fin du Moyen Age*, report delivered at the conference "La Seta in Europa: Secc. XIII-XX", Prato, 4-9 May 1992.

[5]. A. Mancini, U. Dorini, E. Lazzareschi, *Statuto della corte dei mercanti in Lucca del MCCCLXXVI*, Florence, 1927.

[6]. For the production and processing of silk in Venice, see D. Davanzo Poli, *I mestieri della moda a Venezia nei secc. XIII-XVIII. Documenti*, Venice, undated; for Genoa, see P. Massa, *La "Fabbrica" dei velluti genovesi da Genova a Zoagli*, Genoa, 1981.

[7]. A great many documents on marriage dowries have been published; as an example we mention G. Marcotti, *Un mercante fiorentino e la sua famiglia*, Florence, 1881, and G. Biagi, *Due corredi nuziali fiorentini 1320-1423*, Florence, 1899.

[8]. G. Gargiolli, *L'Arte della Seta in Firenze. Trattato del secolo XV*, Florence, 1868: A great part of the essay is dedicated to the dyeing operations. A recent study of the essay in R. Schorta, *Il trattato dell'Arte della Seta. A Florentine 15th Century Treatise on Silk Manufacturing*, in *Bulletin du Cieta*, no. 69, 1991, pgg. 57-86.

[9]. F. Cardini, *I Re Magi di Benozzo Gozzoli*, Florence, 1991.

[10]. F. E. De Roover, *Andrea Banchi Florentine Silk Manufacturer and Merchant in the Fifteenth Century*, in *Studios in Medieval and Renaissance History*, vol. III, Lincoln, 1966, pgg. 221-285.

[11]. R. Morelli, *La seta fiorentina nel Cinquecento*, Milan, 1976.

[12]. F. E. De Roover, *op. cit.*, 1966, pg. 248.

[13]. E. De Roover, *ibid.*, pg. 246.

[14]. E. De Roover, *ibid.*, pg. 285. There were 83 workshops of silk manufacturers in Florence toward the end of the fifteenth century, according to the Chronicle of Benedetto Dei, which is also quoted by De Roover.

[15]. *Omaggio ai Carrand*, Florence, 1989, entry no. 235, edited by R. Orsi Landini; R. Orsi Landini, *Eleonora fra sete e oro*, in *Moda alla corte dei Medici. Gli abiti di Cosimo, Eleonora, Don Garzia restaurati*, exhibition catalogue, Florence, 1993.

[16]. L. Monnas, *The Vestments of Henry VII at Stonyhurst*, in *Bulletin de Liaison du Centre International d'Etude des Textiles Anciens*, no. 65, 1987, pgg. 69-80.

[17]. L. Monnas, *op. cit.*, 1989, pg. 291; Douet D'Arcq, *op. cit.*, 1851, pgg. 13, 110, 157-158, 179.

[18]. For the decorative typologies of fifteenth-century textiles, see R. Bonito Fanelli, P. Peri, *Tessuti italiani del Rinascimento*, exhibition catalogue, Florence, 1981; P. Peri, *Il parato di Niccolò V*, Florence, 1981; *Tessuti serici italiani 1450-1530*, edited by C. Buss, G. Butazzi, M. Molinelli, Milan, 1983; R. De Gennaro, *Velluti operati del secolo XV col motivo delle 'gricce'*, 1, Florence, 1985 and *Velluti operati del XV secolo col motivo 'de' camini'*, Florence, 1987; R. Bonito Fanelli, *Il motivo della melagrana nei tessuti italiani al tempo di Piero della Francesca*, in *Tessuti italiani al tempo di Piero della Francesca*, without indication of place of printing, (Petruzzi editore), 1992, pgg. 36-43. The terms 'griccia' e 'cammino' were often interpreted by the historians as a pattern, while they refer to the different programming of the loom, that these ornamental motifs involve.

[19]. Concerning the sumptuary laws, see R. Levi Pisetzsky, *Storia del costume in Italia*, Milan, vol. II, 1964, pgg. 171 and foll.; P. Molmenti, *La storia di Venezia nella vita privata dalle origini alla caduta della Repubblica*, Bergamo, 2 volumes, IV edition, 1905; I. Del Lungo, *Women of Florence*, London 1907; G. Bistort, *Il magistrato delle pompe nella Repubblica di Venezia*, Bologna, 1912; E. Pandiani, *Vita privata genovese del Rinascimento*, Genoa, 1915; L. Frati, *La vita privata in Bologna dal secolo XIII al XVII*, Bologna, second edition, 1928; D. Roche, *La culture des apparences: Une histoire du vêtement XVIIe-XVIIIe Siécle*, Paris, 1989. C. de Merindol, *Signes de Hierarchie sociale à la fin du Moyen Age d'après le vêtement. Méthodes et recherches*, in A.A.V.V., *Le Vêtement*, *op. cit.*, Paris, 1989.

[20]. L. Portoghesi, *Per una storia del costume nel Seicento umbro*, in *Il costume e l'immagine pittorica nel Seicento umbro*, catalogue of the exhibition at Foligno, Florence, 1984, pg. 17.

[21]. O. Morelli, *Prime riflessioni intorno alla regola del "porre" e del "levare"*, in *Tessuti italiani al tempo di Piero della Francesca*, *op. cit.*, pgg. 80-82.

[22]. For black dyeing in Genoa, see C. Ghiara, *La tintura nera genovese: "La migliore di quante se ne facesse al mondo"*, in *Seta a Genova 1491-1991*, edited by Piera Rum, exhibition catalogue, Genoa, 1991, pgg. 22-28; for the same subject at Florence, R. Orsi Landini, *I paramenti sacri della cappella palatina di Palazzo Pitti*, Florence, 1988, pg. 22; in Venice: R. Berveglieri, *L'arte dei tintori e il nero di Venezia*, in *I mestieri della moda a Venezia dal XIII al XVIII secolo*, exhibition catalogue, Venice, 1988, pgg. 55-61.

Silk Gandin velvet with liseré and pattern wefts.
France, ca. 1900.
Musée Historique des Tissus, Lyon.

FROM THE THRONE TO THE MIDDLE-CLASS PARLOR
Velvets in furnishing and interior decoration

Roberta Orsi Landini

Anonymous, *Touch*, from an engraving in the series, *The Five Senses*, by Abraham Bosse (1602-1676).
Musée de Tours, Tours.

Chair upholstered with ciselé velvet with a pattern typical of the end of sixteenth century.
France, second half of the seventeenth century.
Musée des Arts Décoratifs, Lyon.

Anonymous, *Sight*, from an engraving in the series, *The Five Senses*, by Abraham Bosse (1602-1676).
Musée de Tours, Tours.

Beginning around the middle of the sixteenth century, as Spanish fashion became predominant in Italy, the manufacture of textiles for clothing increasingly tended to develop its own distinctive features, with specific ornamental, technical, and commercial characteristics. On the one hand, the esthetic mechanism that is now so familiar to us – whereby the most important criteria for decision-making in the area of apparel were newness and visual impact – became more and more active and intense. On the other hand, in the manufacture of textiles for the furnishing and decoration of the homes of the aristocratic or simply the well-off, sobriety of ornamentation, along with quality and durability, continued to be the decisive criteria in the selection of a fabric. The key difference between fabrics made to be used in clothing and fabrics made to be used in interior decoration lay in the span of time over which the patterns and the colors were meant to meet with approval by the standards of the prevailing tastes and styles. For the home or the official residence, this span of time was to be calculated not in terms of years, but generations. Velvet continued to be, then – due to the durability of its structure, the amount of silk required, the pleasant sensation derived from its texture as well as its appearance – the most valued fabric for upholstery, used especially for the chairs of particularly important individuals. And, velvet was never again deposed from the thrones of popes and kings, no matter what the fleeting fashion of the moment might happen to be.

The motif of a pomegranate inscribed in an ogive, which appears in its most lavish and elaborate version during the sixteenth century, was developed and adapted to the general shifts in esthetics in an endless array of variations. This was to prove to be a prevailing motif employed in the fabrics that were used from then onward in home furnishings: brocatelles and damasks. Although these types of fabrics continued to win widespread popularity over time – especially the damasks, which were particularly well suited to all sorts of objects and draperies – the velvets used for home furnishing, marked by their powerful and distinctive colors, so often magnificent and rather overstated, did not meet with the same degree of favor in every period. Velvets were promoted by the crowned heads of Europe who were particularly determined to impose fashions and styles that might lead to increases in consumption and competition in the creation of luxury items that would improve the profitability of their royal silk manufactures. Among these sovereigns were Louis XIV, Napoleon I, and Napoleon III. Velvets were instead forgotten during periods in which economic and political setbacks imposed times of discretion and puritanical customs, or when the criteria employed in decoration tended to veer toward lightness and pictorial naturalism.

In the alternation of fashions and styles, an unchallenged position of prominence was to be enjoyed by the velvets for home furnishing, with two, three, or more pile warps of different colors, known in Italy as "velluti a giardino", the pride of Genoan manufacturers. These velvets are manufactured according to techniques used for the polychromatic velvets first woven from the XIV century on. While the latter were often made of solid cut pile, in the very finest velvets "a giardino" of the seventeenth and eighteenth centuries, the ground is voided, often white with a silver lamella weft; the pattern, in cut and uncut pile, was adapted to the prevailing style, whether that meant that it was to be full-bodied and monumental, or at other times more delicate and naturalistic. Though the most valuable of these velvets were those manufactured in Genoa[1], all of the major silk manufactories, and not only those in Italy, produced them up until the middle of the eighteenth century. With time, they

Canapé upholstered in *a giardino* velvet.
Apartment of Madame du Barry, the library. Versailles.
Musée Nationale, Versailles.

became classic features in the furnishings of aristocratic palaces and homes, and they were taken up again at the end of the nineteenth century by the Italian manufactories, which were striving to revive antique fabrics[2]. These velvets still figure in the sample lines of the firms that are keeping the art of manual weaving alive.

During the seventeenth century, the uncontested Italian leadership in the manufacture of silks ended; Lyon, as well as Paris and Tours, began to produce fabrics of extremely high quality. When Louis XIV decided to create a setting incomparable luxury around his royal person – setting an example and encouraging his own citizens and foreign courts to consume French products, which had become synonymous with fashionability and elegance – he went on to finance and promote the success of the so-called Grande Fabrique, or Great Factory, of Lyon. In the space of just a few decades, in part through the development of a new wave of design in the fabrics, French silks won a position of uncontested supremacy, a reputation that had once belonged to the Italian manufactories. Artists and designers of illustrious renown designed the fabrics that were to be used in royal palaces. Among them was Jean Berain, who was responsible for some of the most handsome velvets for furnishing designed in that century. In accordance with the high-flown tastes typical of the style of Louis XIV, the motifs with wide pattern unit broke completely with the sixteenth-century style, tending toward a vertical succession of distinct levels, with the introduction of such innovative features as cornices, baldachins, exotic figures, and sphinxes. The colors employed were royal reds and dark greens; at times however the monumental nature of the designs were lightened with delicate pastel shades, which increased the value of the fabric because of the enormous technical difficulties of weaving them while still keeping the silk pile "clean", without shadings or stripings. With the advent of the Louis XIV style, the fabrics of the Grande Fabrique of Lyon attained a position of uncontested leadership throughout Europe, in terms of quality of design and technical refinement, a position that endured until the twentieth century.

The eighteenth century was the period that least favored velvet upholstery: in that century there was a clear tendency toward silks with bright, light shades, and less heavy, though they might be extremely rich and complex, with great quantities of extremely fine gold and silver wefts. In this period there was a clear tendency to imitate the effect of the pile, with the invention of a new type of yarn, the chenille. From the middle of the century on, chenille was used to enrich the inimitable French brocades. Velvet was even banished from the royal apartments, and was replaced by satins and lampas decorated with bouquets of flowers, panoramic views, undulating laces, and trellises. Only polychrome velvet managed to carve out a place for itself in this century, or at least to be accepted within the context of a taste that drew its inspiration from nature, elevating to a central position all of the nuances of color and unpredictable forms. More than for the broad surfaces of wall coverings, or for the upholstery of chairs and canapés, the effects of cut and uncut pile, with one or more pile warps of different colours met with favor in the production of borders. Beginning in the middle of the century, these uses acquired increasing importance in the welter of decorative fabrics used for interior decoration. At times they were produced on narrow looms, but they were often woven in two, four or six together on one regular width of cloth, which was then cut lengthwise into strips. The importance of edges and hems in interior decoration reached its culmination during the Empire period.

Used sparingly in homes, velvet proved to be the covering material of choice in the interiors of carriages, where it was used to

Silk ciselé velvet with two pile warps and a laminated ground. England, Spitalfields, second half of the eighteenth century. Museo del Tessuto e del Costume Storico, Spoleto.

Silk ciselé velvet with the
initials of the French Republic.
Lyon, Chatel and Tassinari
Manufactory, 1900.
Musée Historique des Tissus,
Lyon.

Silk cut voided velvet with the
emblem of the House of
Savoy, manufactured for the
royal train.
Florence, Giuseppe Lisio
Manufactory, ca. 1930.
Lisio Arte della Seta
Foundation, Florence.

On page 56:
Silk ciselé velvet with three
pile warps.
Florence, Giuseppe Lisio
Manufactory, manufactured
from 1925 on.
Lisio Arte della Seta
Foundation, Florence.

Ciselé velvet with two pile warps.
Genoa, second half of the seventeenth century.
Musée Historique des Tissus, Lyon.

Chiné velvet, made for Versailles.
Lyon, Grand Frères Manufactory, 1811-1813.
Mobilier National, Paris.

Silk ciselé velvet woven for the Hotel de la Paiva in Paris.
Lyon, 1873.
Musée Historique des Tissus, Lyon.

Ciselé velvet with a laminated ground.
Lyon, Bissardon, Cousin et Bony Manufactory, 1811-1813.
Mobilier National, Paris.

upholster walls and to cover cushions. Aside from its esthetic value, velvet was unquestionably very durable, and it served to insulate and pad; for these reasons it was by far the favourite material for these specific purposes. In the eighteenth century, velvets for carriages were accorded a specific manufacturing area all their own. Their motifs were influenced by velvets for clothing, which generally tended toward a fine and asymmetrical reticule. Since that time, the success of these fabrics for the upholstery of vehicles and means of transport has never flagged, especially as solid velvets.

The French Revolution, which sharply diminished the demand for luxury goods, cast a shadow over the future of the Grande Fabrique of Lyon; the factory recovered thanks to the enlightened policies of Napoleon I[3]. The emperor, with the two-fold purpose of reviving the silk manufactories (which were prostrated by the economic effects of the wars) and of creating a setting of luxury suitable to the image of power and magnificence worthy of the foremost sovereign of Europe, promoted – with huge commissions – the production of all of the precious fabrics for which France had long been renowned.

Production of all of the most lavish fabrics, therefore, began anew: lavish in terms of yarns, technical quality, and types of design. The goal was that of creating an inimitable imperial style. Among the various fabrics, velvet conquered a position that was, if not preeminent, certainly of great prestige, as we can see from the splendid pieces of work that were commissioned for Versailles, and which are still preserved. They are velvets with an ample pattern unit, in some cases brocaded with gold wefts, in other cases woven in such a way as to leave areas of voided ground that were then filled in with embroidery. In the early years of the nineteenth century, the Grand Frères manufactory, heir to the prestigious manufacturing operation of Camille Pernon, produced a velvet with some extraordinary properties for the royal residence. Alongside the complex technique of "chiné" used to trace the decorative motif onto the surface of the pile, the velvet has a double width and a ground in white pile.

Keeping the most prestigious manufactories running – and the overall image of French silk production was entrusted to the marvelous silks of Lyon – had been a specific objective of the policies of Napoleon. The emperor had, moreover, a lively and unflagging interest in technical innovations of all kinds, and he understood very clearly that the future success of the manufacturers depended on quality on the speed and pace of production, as well as the modernization of the manufacturing facilities. The application of the Jacquard mechanism to the looms, which eliminated the job of the drawboy – first tested in 1804 and then spread at a growing rate through the later years of the empire – proved to be a decisive factor in the success of the French textile industry. From the 1820s onward, research and experimentation in machinery and systems, designed to make manufacturing cheaper or to create special effects and finishes, proceeded at a remarkably rapid and fruitful pace, assisted by the stimulus provided by awards, and by the regular series of national and international expositions, where the latest technical advances could be explained and propagated.

The manufacturing of velvet, which had once again become popular, especially for use in clothing, urgently required more flexible and rapid systems of production. Research and experimentation pointed in two main directions: either the construction of looms which could weave two fabrics simultaneously face to face, with a single pile warp cut during weaving; or else the production of a fabric with a pile surface created not by an extra warp, but by the

Fernand Pelez de Cordova, *Salon from the Period of the Second Empire*, 1862.
Galleria Nazionale d'Arte Moderna, Mario Praz Collection, Rome.

cutting of floats of the weft. Velvets were therefore the subject of extensive experimentation, well documented in the Dictionnaire général des tissus du Bezon, published in the mid-nineteenth century. In that work, the treatment of the types of velvet produced in France occupies no fewer than three volumes; there are descriptions not only of the new manufacturing techniques, but also of an infinite variety of new styles and types, which the industry was crowding onto the markets in rapid succession in an effort to promote demand.

Figured hand-cut velvets of excellent quality continued, nonetheless, to be produced throughout the century, while the new types produced by industry with the latest techniques – either solid or corduroy, for the most part – spread everywhere. Alongside the more modern systems of production there was the use of materials that had not been employed in the production of velvet prior to the nineteenth century. The mechanical spinning of cotton made it possible to obtain extremely fine and regular yarns that ensured excellent results with double piece or weft-pile velvets. In the field of textiles, then, the first half of the nineteenth century proved to be extremely fertile in terms of technological development; up until the 1840s, on the other hand, the whole matter of design of the fabrics was neglected. Models taken from the styles of a more or less recent past were constantly reused, though there was some borrowing of ideas from the Near and the Far East.

The advantages of velvet in interior decoration became increasingly appreciated during the Second Empire, due to the increases in production brought about by revolutions in manufacturing systems and the reduction in costs prompted both by mechanization and by the wider use of cotton. The darker colors – deep reds and greens – were used widely to create dramatic and absorbing atmospheres, to ennoble the sumptuous homes of the powerful new middle class. Those same homes happily accepted even the precious items that the industrialists of Lyon proposed: hand-woven with large-scale drawings, in the style of Berain that had been so beloved by Louis XIV.

From the middle of the nineteenth century on, textiles had acquired a role of fundamental importance in interior decorating[+]. not so much as a manifestation of wealth or as the chief medium of decoration (as was the case throughout the eighteenth century or during the Empire period), but rather in terms of comfort. In private rooms and in reception areas, the presence of curtains, shades, padded furniture, and tablecloths became intrusive and predominant. The home, which was officially considered to be the realm of the woman, was in fact the realm of the woman's upholsterer – women's periodicals and the other new trade publications worked together to suggest unbelievable and unprecedented forms and shapes for draperies and coverings for "capitoné" furniture, with entirely new shapes, rotund and allusive. There was no effort to establish a single overall style, nor was there the slightest need for a programmatic coordination of the fabrics that invaded the home, covering all, cushioning the corners of every object, and symbolically padding the sharp edges of life. Velvet – warm, soft, and sensual – was the most comfortable fabric available, as well as the fabric that best personified the nineteenth-century idea of the home as a haven.

Even patterned velvet with classic designs found an important place in the homes of the late nineteenth century. The historical taste of the period brought figured velvet back into favor, with the incessant revisitation of all styles, in a search for cultural identity all its own. While the time of Louis XIV was the source of inspiration for

Robert Lèfevre, *Marie Pauline*, ca. 1812.
Musée National du Chateau, Versailles.

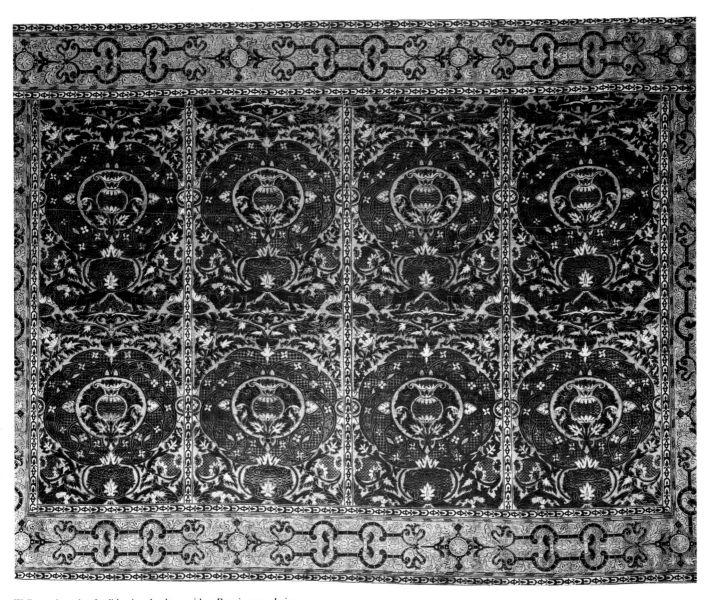

Wall panel made of solid printed velvet, with a Renaissance design.
Venice, Mariano Fortuny y Madrazo, first quarter of the twentieth century.
Formerly in the collection of Liana and Carlo Carnevali, Florence.

Gandin velvet with liseré and pattern wefts.
Lyon, ca. 1900.
Musée Historique des Tissus, Lyon.

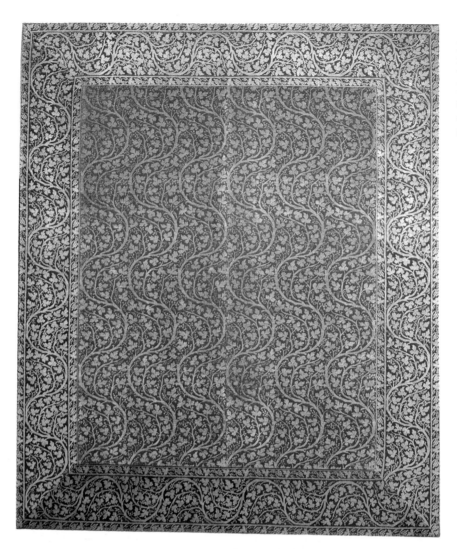

Furnishing panel made of solid printed velvet, with a fourteenth-century design.
Venice, Mariano Fortuny y Madrazo, first quarter of the twentieth century.
Collection of Liana and Carlo Carnevali, Florence.

Cushion made of solid printed velvet, with a seventeenth-century design.
Venice, Mariano Fortuny y Madrazo, first quarter of the twentieth century.
Fortuny Museum, Venice.

On page 65:
Decorative panel made of solid printed velvet, presented at the exposition of the Roman secession in 1915.
Rome, Maria Monaci Gallenga, ca. 1915.
Collection of Liana and Carlo Carnevali, Florence.

velvet in France, in Italy the Renaissance was the model. Alongside the new textile factories being founded during the last years of the century, with modern techniques and machinery (mainly imported from Germany – as in the case of the Redaelli company of Mandello del Lario), others were being established to produce not only the motifs of older fabrics, but also the older weaving techniques. Velvet was once again made on hand-operated looms; industrialists began collections of historical fabrics with a view to reproducing them faithfully, much like what had happened in France. Looms for the production of velvet by hand were set up by Luigi Ardizzoni in Genoa, Guglielmo Ghidini in Turin, Carlo Fumagalli and Vittorio Ferrari in Milan, and Luigi Bevilacqua and Lorenzo Rubelli in Venice[5]. The production of fabrics, with designs based on Renaissance patterns and manufactured with traditional techniques, found extremely fertile territory for research and experimentation in the eclectic taste of the nineteenth century. This style allowed for the coexistence of different styles, and introduced with growing frequency authentic antique furniture in home furnishing. Moreover, the new market for the restoration and reconstruction of historical

ations of a people's culture, elevating them to the rank of art forms, they felt that they were involved in a great renewal that was sweeping through all areas of crafts and industrial production, with wonderful results; this gave rise to a single style, known in France as Art Nouveau. The principles of ornamentation became the subject of studies and treatises; the specific problems of textile decoration and those involved in a search for harmonious modularity were intriguing and attractive to the artists of the time. These problems constituted a field of research in which the transition from artistic product to industrial product could occur[6]. Although the personalities and the interests of the individual artists may have differed considerably, as did the spirits of the nations and the various schools, all found that they basically agreed on the need to search for two-dimensional models in which abstraction and the stylized figuration of natural forms could be melded. The discovery of Japanese painting and drawing, which constituted the fundamental building block in the iconographic renewal then underway, led these pioneers to study the value of the line, of empty and full spaces, and of geometric composition, with a de facto abolition of all and any

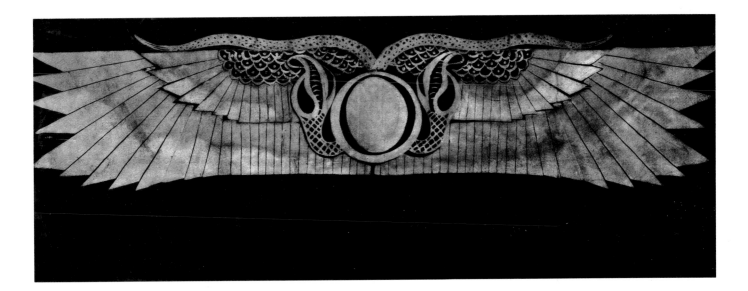

residences was opening up rapidly in this particular period.

Production of fabrics in the Renaissance style continued, at any rate, well beyond the turn of the century. Outside of Italy as well, it continued to survive, alongside the great esthetic renovations of the twentieth century, following its own elitist, parallel course, staking out as its territory the function of balancing and rationalizing every excess of taste and fashions. It was in this same spirit, for that matter, that William Morris studied the Italian fabrics of the fifteenth century, in his experimental search for a new esthetic language to set up in opposition to the bad taste of the Victorian era. From the theories developed by English artistic circles, and from the work of Walter Crane and of Lewis F. Day – the first theorist of industrial design for textiles – but above all from the discovery of Japanese art, new esthetic criteria emerged that revolutionized the tastes of the era and, as a result, the nature of decorative textiles.

From the 1870s onward, artists from various European nations once again began to turn their attention to the rooms and objects that formed the basis of daily life. Influenced by the atmosphere of positivism, which assigned new values to the material manifest-

interest in the plastic potential of fabrics. Velvet, too, was therefore inevitably perceived and treated as a flat surface; the decorations employed had little to do with the structure of the velvet, but rather with the creation of printed motifs. Printing upon velvet was at the time done with traditional systems, using wooden or metal block prints, until the invention, in the early years of the twentieth century, of the procedure of silk screening[7]. Velvets were generally produced on double velvet looms, a technique in which the German textiles industry had been gaining expertise and importance around the year 1870. Aside from the fact that they possessed the technological resources required to ensure that the resulting textiles would be of high quality, the Germans also succeeded in developing their own decorative style, with the creative assistance of the finest architects and designers of the period. Among them, Henry Van de Velde was the first to be assigned commissions from the silk manufactories of Krefeld. In the earliest years of the century, under Van de Velde's influence, other German artists as well worked to provide the textiles industry with models, and they too tended toward abstract curvilinear motifs, which later evolved into an original

Silk cut voided velvet with two pile warps and liseré wefts.
Florence, Giuseppe Lisio Manufactory, manufactured from 1925 on.
Lisio Arte della Seta Foundation, Florence.

Ciselé velvet with two pile warps.
Italy, ca. 1920. Private collection, Venice.

Ciselé velvet with two pile warps.
Italy, ca. 1925. Private collection, Venice.

visual language based on small, two-dimensional geometric designs.

While the French school of design adopted the new ornamental themes of the late nineteenth century, thus remaining bound to their own naturalistic and floral design tradition, with its emphatic style and a tendency toward the creation of lavish fabrics, the artists of German-speaking countries opted for a more rational approach to design. Adolf Loos, in Vienna, became the spokesman for a decisive rejection of all forms of decorativism, drawing up projects for interior decoration in a simplified and essential style. Small geometric patterns, particularly suited to the needs of modern industry, harmonized perfectly with the linear and functional designs of new furniture.

Velvet, made of traditional materials or with innovative formulas, found new and far wider possibilities for application in the seating in public facilities, in theaters and later in movie houses, in railway carriages and in the interiors of airplanes. With a solid wool pile, sometimes with printed decorations, velvet proved to be a remarkably durable, comfortable type of fabric, with excellent properties of insulation.

It was toward the end of the Twenties that the unusual esthetic qualities of velvet, bound up with its three-dimensional nature, were once again cast into the spotlight. The new esthetic canons, introduced by the artistic avant-gardes, especially Cubism and Futurism, found special possibilities of expression in velvet. After many years of two-dimensional decoration, in which line, color, and prints were the uncontested areas of textiles design, texture, different levels and planes, and the manifold refraction of light which could be generated by variations in the weave, once again became territories for experimentation and research, with a view to reproduction through mechanical systems. The modern visual language, which involved breaking down the various planes and the depiction of vital dynamism, were translated into the design of velvets with radically new patterns and motifs and equally new techniques of production. The various effects of shape and lighting that could be produced by uncut and cut pile, or different materials, prompted new technical inventions. It became possible to produce double "ciselé" velvets, in which the brilliance of the new artificial yarns were balanced against the opaque warmth of organic fibers. The nuanced effects of airbrushing, which were typical of the print fabrics of the Thirties, could be translated into velvet with the use of two different piles that varied in nature or in color, by merging one into the other, so as to accentuate the shape and dynamic qualities of the design.

New experimentation into special aspects of velvet – and of course of other figured fabrics – was to a great extent the work of the artists of the Bauhaus, who were championing a renewal that went beyond the areas of design and touched on the morphological qualities and potential of the product. A purely decorative visual language, which was still used by the majority of European and American textiles manufacturers, was being replaced by a functional and rationalist idiom: form, color, and material were to be integrated with one another, corresponding reciprocally in harmonious unity. In the experimental workshop of the Bauhaus in Weimar, textiles were developing in the context of the designs of interior decoration and furnishing being developed by Gropius, Mies Van der Rohe, and Breuer. The fabrics were analyzed in their physical qualities as materials, and in their capacities to reflect or absorb light and sound. The structure of the weave tended therefore to become a fundamental decorative criterion.

Hector Guimard, Detail of a chair, ca. 1904.
(Mark Vokar Editeur. Paris)

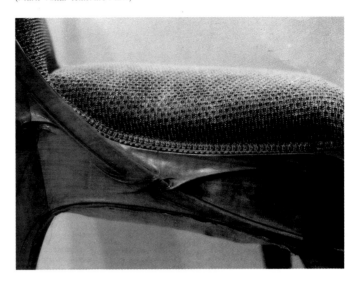

Victor Horta, Solvay Home, easy chair.
(Academy Editions, London)

Ciselé velvet with two pile warps.
Italy, 1920-1930.
Private collection, Venice.

Georges De Feure, Chair and padded canapé.
(Mark Vokar Editeur, Paris)

Henry Van de Velde, Chair, 1898.
(Thames and Hudson, London)

Interior of a railway carriage
designed by George Mortimer Pullman, 1859.
(Mallard Press, New York)

Interior of a Grand Confort carriage.
Italian State Railways, 1988.

Detail of the interior
of a car on the Orient Express.
(ETR, Salò)

Carlo Mollino, Casa Rivetti, dining room
and detail of the bedroom.
(Idea Books Edizioni, Milan)

During those years, there also developed a new role for the designer, very distant from that of the turn of the century, when the designer was uninterested in industrial production, considered vulgar and incapable of generating beauty. Design was declared to be at the service of industry, taking into account and making the best possible use of the possibilities and potential of machinery and the newest scientific discoveries in the fields of chemistry and the invention of new artificial and synthetic fibers. While technological innovation remained secondary to the esthetic results in the area of the manufacture of textiles for clothing, in the field of furnishing the functionalist criteria expressed during the Thirties continued to develop in modern production. New weaves and materials were developed as a function of the use to which the product being manufactured was to be put; textiles acquired new qualities that would have been unthinkable only a few years previously – they became stain-proof, wrinkle-proof, and fire-proof. Among all of the fabrics now being produced for all sorts of interiors, including the interiors of vehicles, velvet remains unquestionably the most compliant in terms of adaptability to specific requirements. It is easy to vary weave, fiber quality and pile depth. Moreover, it combines its unique esthetic characteristics with natural and easily acquired technical properties.

Notes

[1]. M. Bezon, *Dictionnaire général des tissus anciens et modernes*, Lyon, ed. Th. Lepagnez, second edition, vol. II, 1859, pgg. 89-94.

[2]. Concerning the nineteenth-century revival of Genoese fabrics in Genoa, see M.R. Montiani Bensi, *La produzione della manifattura genovese Ardizzoni*, in *Le tappezzerie nelle dimore storiche. Studi e metodi di conservazione*, Proceedings of the conference of Florence, Turin, 1987.

[3]. Concerning Napoleon's policies in favor of the manufacturers of Lyon, see J. Coural, *Paris, Mobilier National. Soieries Empire. Inventaire des collections publiques françaises*. Paris, 1980; *Le sete impero dei palazzi napoleonici*, exhibition catalogue, Florence, 1988; R. Orsi Landini, *Le sete francesi del periodo neoclassico e impero. Prodotto e immagine*, in *Il tessuto nell'eta' del Canova*, edited by Marta Cuoghi Costantini, Milan, 1992, pgg. 15-35.

[4]. Concerning the interiors of the nineteenth century, see the classic work: M. Praz, *La filosofia dell'arredamento*, Milan, 1981; P. Thornton, *Il gusto della casa: storia per immagini dell'arredamento 1620-1920*, Milan, 1984; (edited by) A. Zanni, *Mobili soffici*, Milan, 1990, with accompanying bibliography.

[5]. From L. Brenni, *I velluti di seta italiani*, Milan, 1927.

[6]. Concerning the fabrics of the twentieth century, see the studies by G. and R. Fanelli, *Il tessuto moderno Disegno Moda Architettura 1890-1940*, Florence, 1976; *Il Tessuto Art Deco e Anni Trenta*, Florence; *Il tessuto Art Nouveau Disegno Moda Architettura*, Florence, 1986.

[7]. G. e R. Fanelli, *Il tessuto Art Déco*, op. cit., pg. 177.

Interior with Etro furnishing fabrics.

Homage to Carlo Mollino, Ardea, Zanotta easy chair.

Achille Castiglioni, easy chair/bed, Polet, Interflex.

Massimo Iosa Ghini, easy chair, Moroso.

Masanori Umeda, Getsuen easy chair, Edra.

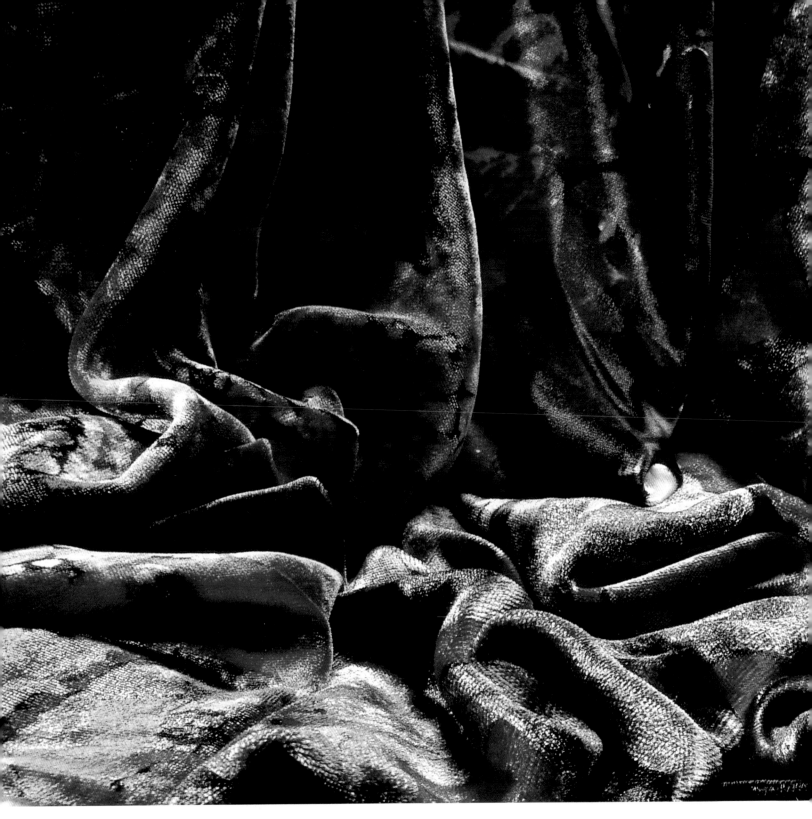

LUXURY AND PRACTICALITY

The thousand faces of velvet for clothing

Roberta Orsi Landini

Prospero Fontana, *Portrait of a Gentlewoman*, ca. 1540.
Museo Davia Bargellini, Bologna.

Moretto da Brescia
Portrait of Count Sciarra Martinengo Cesaresco, 1526.
The National Gallery, London.

From the second half of the sixteenth century onward, the manufacture of textiles gradually came to acquire varied and specific characteristics, according to the use to which those textiles were to be put. Changes in line and cut, prompted by the Spanish influence on clothing styles and by the cultural climate of the Counter Reformation, led to a stiffening in terms of the overall tailoring. This resulted in clothing that tended to mask, conceal, and disguise the lines of the body.

Modesty, the prime virtue of every Christian, clearly clashed with clothing made of excessively flashy fabrics. The marks of status and rank, though still bound up with the quantity of silk and gold arrayed upon the clothing, began to be expressed through the exquisite refinement of ornamentation, and from the middle of the seventeenth century onward, those marks of distinction began to evolve into the dictates of fashion, which changed with growing rapidity.

During the sixteenth century, velvets maintained their leadership among luxury fabrics, but they clearly came to be considered fabrics for use during the winter. Their use was preferred for heavy vests, outerwear, capes, hats, and muffs, all of which were often finished or lined with precious furs. Often plain velvets, with cut or solid uncut pile[1] – no longer forbidden by sumptuary laws – were used, and were in time ennobled by embroideries, slashes, and appliques. In figured velvets, the motifs became progressively smaller. Until the end of the century, they maintained their symmetrical grid structure, which tended to enclose a simplified version of the typical sixteenth-century floral motif, or a small flowering vase.

Alongside this sort of decoration, a well consolidated standard in traditional textiles, another ornamental type appeared at the end of the sixteenth century, which had been specifically conceived for clothing: the so-called design "a mazze", meaning "mace design"[2]. This motif of a little pattern unit was constituted by straight bars with two inflorescences, one above and one below, arranged in an alternating checkerboard pattern, half facing one way and half the other. Often the specific design of the pattern allowed the fabric to have no specific upper or lower side, thus making it possible to join swatches in such a way as to avoid waste, a detail that was particularly well suited to the production of the cone-shaped gowns that had come into fashion in that period. With the softening of styles and with the preference that was increasingly being accorded to rounded and dynamic shapes, the "mace" gradually turned into an S-shaped arrangement[3] or into an elegant little branch with a curly stem, better suited to the artistic canons of the new century. The tulip, the flower of the seventeenth century, was often inserted among the daffodils, carnations, and lilies that were so typical of the Renaissance tradition.

The popularity that this type of pattern enjoyed kept them in fashion for over half a century, during which time they were interpreted in various forms by all of the manufactories, and produced in a wide variety of colors[4] and techniques. In the context of the velvets that were manufactured for use in clothing, in particular, the smaller size of the design module, which allowed a more rapid shift in the programming of the looms, prompted the weavers to engage in experimentation with every effect imaginable, and to work to develop new esthetic and technical innovations. The most popular type became that of "ciselé" velvets, which featured loops and tufts. The combinations among the two types of pile, and the relationships among those types and the ground, gave rise to fabrics with different appearances and qualities of light and weight. In the traditional formula, the motif was made of tufts of cut pile on a

Silk ciselé velvet.
Italy, ca. 1580-1600.
Musée Historique des
Tissus, Lyon.

Silk ciselé velvet.
Italy, ca. 1580-1600.
Musée Historique des
Tissus, Lyon.

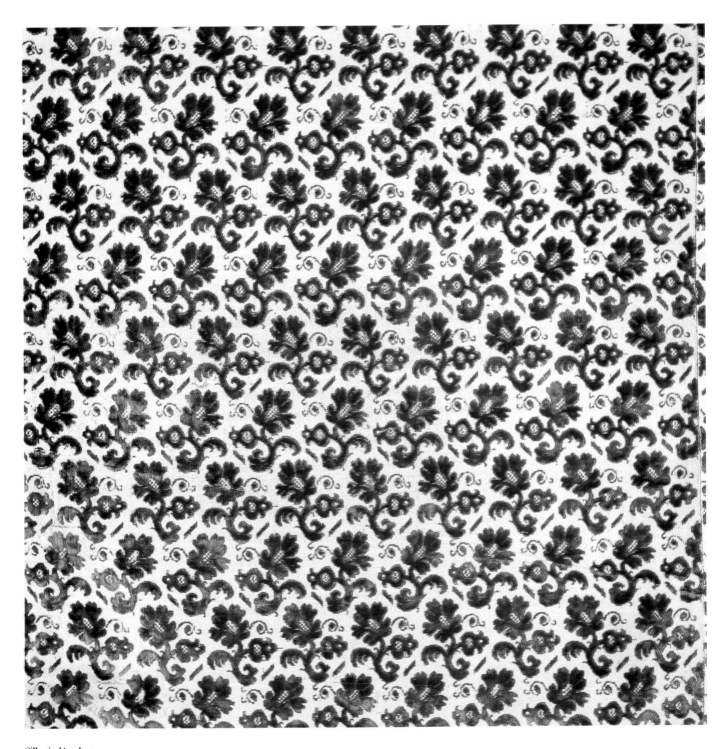

Silk ciselé velvet.
Italy, first quarter of the seventeenth century.
Museo del Tessuto e del Costume Storico, Spoleto.

Solid cut stamped velvet.
Italy, end of the sixteenth
century/beginning of the seventeenth
century.
Collection of the Lisio Arte della Seta
Foundation, Florence.

Silk ciselé velvet.
Italy, first quarter of the seventeenth
century.
Collection of the Lisio Arte della Seta
Foundation, Florence.

ground usually in satin. The uncut pile surrounded it in a fine line that was of lower height and which had a distinctive luminous tone, so as to create an intermediate passage which made the decoration practically a bas-relief. But the plastic qualities of the fabric were no longer the prime consideration of the weaver, who was now intent on composing planes of varied luminosity. At times the weaver would reverse the relationships, designing the motif in reverse so that it would appear to be carved out of the pile; or else the weaver would give prevalence to the areas in uncut pile, or trace two different patterns, using two or three different levels of the fabric. In some cases, the ground never appears at all and the motif (in uncut pile on a ground of cut pile, or vice versa) became visible only through the way the light struck the velvet. The fabric was therefore designed with emphasis given not only to the pattern but also to its overall appearance, with due consideration to the fact that it was being worn by a body in movement, so that the lighting and the shades of color changed as it moved. The peak of refinement in this sort of velvet was attained in the use of black upon black. Gold grounds continued to be used for velvet, though the presence of gold or silver became increasingly discreet: gold fiber weft went from selvage to selvage, rather than being woven in fabulously expensive brocade effects. Instead of using gold thread, formed by an extremely fine lamella wrapped around a silk core, a simple gilded metal strip was usually inserted, making the fabric much lighter and making it possible to save a considerable quantity of the precious metal, as well as hours of labor. The fine strip of gold, which was more delicate than gold and silver "filé" thread, tended to break easily, but the need for finding less costly systems of production that did not tie up great amounts of capital became an increasingly pressing imperative, the more rapidly fashions changed. The manufacture of silk was no longer a preferred field of investment for major fortunes, which now tended to be invested in real estate. Producing the maximum appearance at the minimum cost became the rule for silk manufacturers.

The need to save on raw materials and on manufacturing time led to the creation of new sorts of textiles, and among these the most interesting was gauffered or stamped velvet. Special finishes obtained after weaving had been widely practiced for many years, foremost among them the "moiré" effect; likewise, hot pressing with metal rollers and blocks is documented in the sixteenth and seventeenth centuries, even on such plain fabrics as taffetas[5]. This process produced depressions on the surface of the cloth, creating a pattern or motif.

In the search for new types, with a view to expanding and stimulating the market, the different heights to which it was possible to cut the pile proved to be a particularly fertile area of experimentation. Slashes in clothing, for example, practiced according to styles which incurred the wrath of magistrates, tended to produce decorative fringes around the cuts themselves. The velvet manufacturers succeeded in imitating those cuts, producing fabrics that were both in accordance with the sumptuary laws and the dictates of elegance. The false slashes had the appearance of small tufts that were much longer than the normal pile of velvet, that formed the motif of the fabric; they were then implemented with special velvet rods of considerable height. This may have been the idea that gave rise to the manufacture of plush, a sort of velvet with a very long pile[6]. Beginning in this period, plushes were made in a great many variants, including fibers other than silk[7].

Until around the middle of the seventeenth century, there was no gender-based differentiation practiced in the use of velvet in

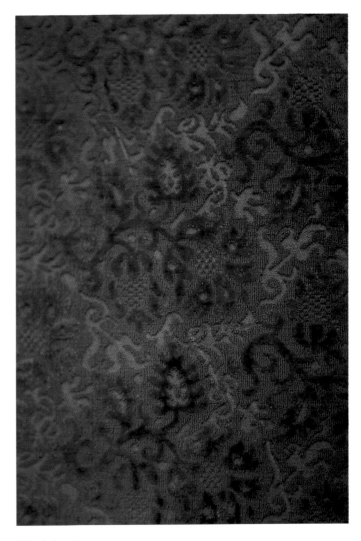

Silk ciselé velvet.
Italy, first quarter of the seventeenth century.
Collection of the Lisio Arte
della Seta Foundation, Florence.

Silk uncut voided velvet, with a plush
effect.
Italy, first quarter of the seventeenth
century.
Musée Historique des Tissus, Lyon.

Silk ciselé velvet.
Italy, first quarter of the seventeenth
century.
Musée Historique des Tissus, Lyon.

French school, *The Regent Philippe d'Orléans in his study
with his son, the Duke of Chartres.*
Beginning of the eighteenth century.
Musée National du Chateau, Versailles.

Silk ciselé velvet with two pile
warps and a laminated ground (miniature velvet).
France, third quarter of the eighteenth century.
Musée Historique des Tissus, Lyon.

Man's suit in silk ciselé velvet.
Venetian manufactory (?), ca. 1750.
Galleria del Costume, Florence.

Silk ciselé velvet.
France, third quarter of the eighteenth century.
Collection of the Lisio Arte
della Seta Foundation, Florence.

clothing, just as there were no substantial gender-based differences in the choice of motifs and colors. Black, like pink, could be as readily chosen by a cavalier as by a lady, in a solid or in a figured velvet. In the process of creating an increasingly specialized and differentiated array of products, a process that had been triggered by the mechanism of fashion and directed toward stimulating an increasingly rapid and extensive spread of consumption, velvet acquired the connotation of being a fabric used predominantly by men. After the first decades of the seventeenth century, women's clothing became softer in form, in contrast with the austere and chaste apparel of the turn of the century; ladies were more generous in the glimpses they allowed of their charms, and those glimpses were nuanced by the use of fabrics with softer and more enfolding drapery. For a long period, ladies preferred to use lighter fabrics for their clothing, with brighter colors and more complex designs, attained through other weaving techniques, save in capes and other items typically worn in winter. Men's clothing, on the other hand, began to be codified toward the end of the century into a set of three items (coat, waistcoat, and breeches). In order to be considered elegant, clothing had to maintain its shape; the more straight and essential lines of this clothing required a fabric with a solid weave. Often men's vanity found its expression in the selection of a waistcoat made of fabrics with an incredibly lavish gold brocading effects, revealed only in part by the coat made of solid silk velvet. Heavy gold and silk embroidery or the application of broad braidery often served to decorate a dress suit, required in appearances at court. In the eighteenth century, embroidery was widely used in men's fashion, on solid velvets, but also on figured ones.

An entire specific sector of manufacturing served to produce velvets with smaller motifs, intended for men's clothing. Toward the middle of the century, in accordance with the designs of light and dynamic fashions then in vogue, the decorations became asymmetrical and far more lively. If they were produced with extremely sophisticated techniques (with two or three pile warps often with "lamé" ground), they were dubbed "miniature velvets"[8]. In that case, the clothing did not require further work from the embroiderer in order to be considered sufficiently lavish. Toward the middle of the eighteenth century, the manufactories of Lyon – which enjoyed an uncontested leadership in the sector of clothing, and which dictated fashion throughout Europe – launched, as the greatest possible mark of elegance, fabrics woven to shape, in which the design was arranged according to the shape of the article of clothing that was to be made with it. The motif was more lavish in the front, where the buttons were to be placed; it followed the shape of the neck and the hem of the coat and waistcoat; it followed the form of the pocket flaps and the cuffs. The overall effect, even when the technique of production was a precious "ciselé" velvet, was less ostentatious than a flashy embroidery in gold or silver; nonetheless, in elegant circles, the worth of a fabric with so broad a pattern unit was lost on no one. It is a style that inevitably indicates with its appearance a florid economic state, but which disappeared from clothing when economic conditions began to change. Clothing made with velvets woven to shape enjoyed a brief period of popularity in France prior to the Revolution, after which tastes shifted toward men's clothing with smaller patterns, very well suited to adornment with naturalistic or neoclassical decorations.

Velvet unfailingly maintained a prominent place in the pomp and regalia surrounding sovereigns over the centuries; the uniforms of those who were closest to the king were meant to be the most lavish in a hierarchy of appearance very similar to the distribution of jobs

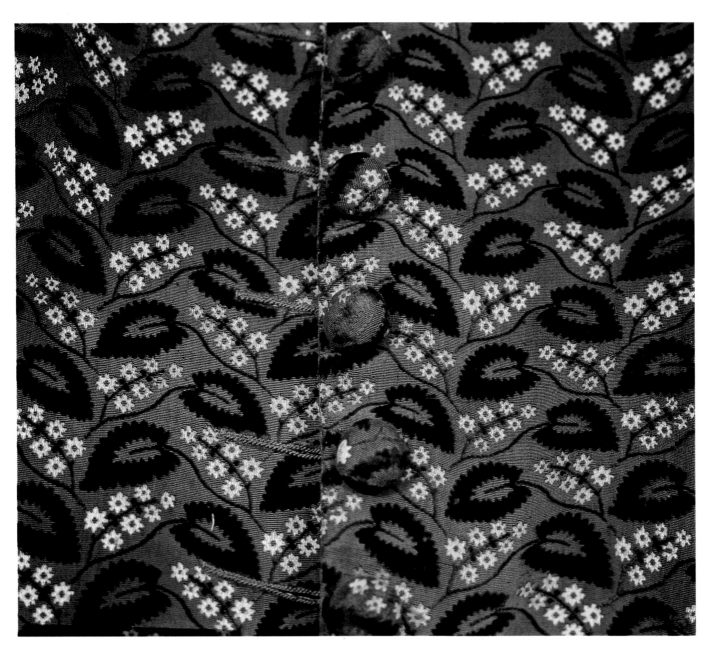

Silk cicelé velvet.
France, third quarter of the eighteenth century.
Musée Historique des Tissus, Lyon.

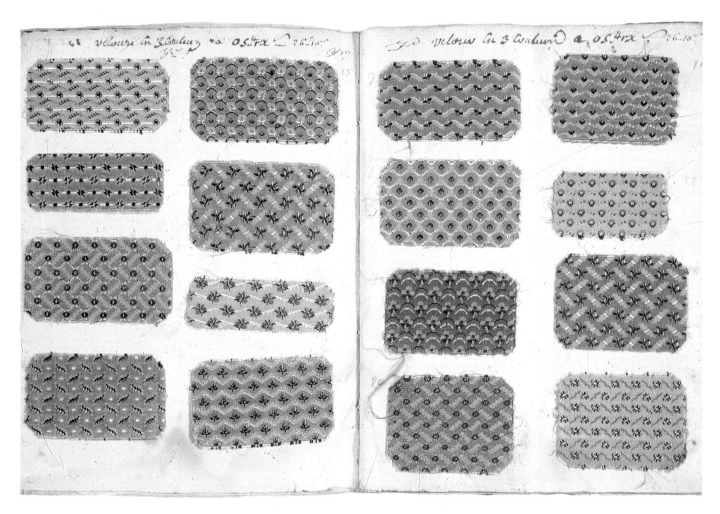

Array of samples, with examples of miniature velvets.
France (?), first quarter of the eighteenth century.
Museo Correr, Venice.

Miniature velvet.
France, third quarter of the eighteenth century.
Musée Historique des Tissus, Lyon.

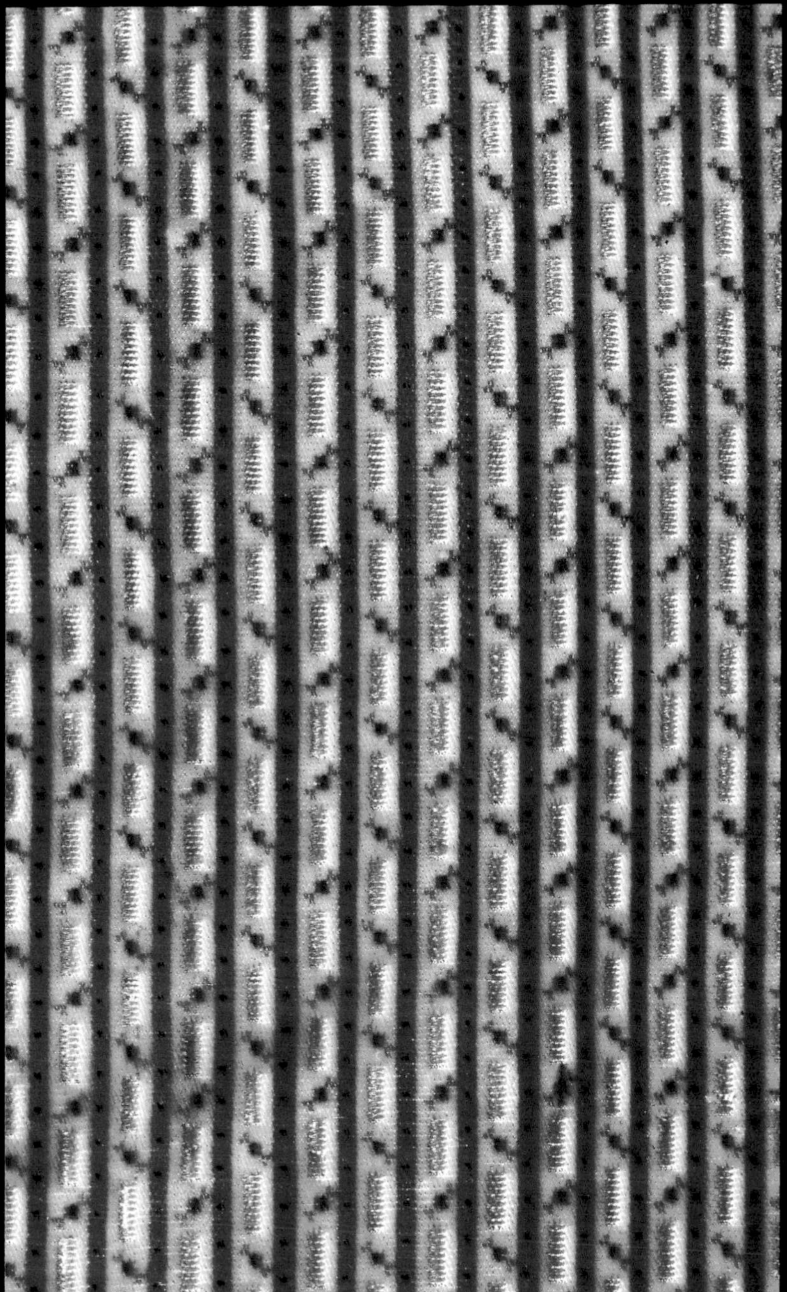

Court mantle in silk velvet with gold embroidery, worn by the Princess de Léon at Napoleon's second wedding.
France, ca. 1810.
The Metropolitan Museum of Art, New York.

Suit made of solid silk velvet with silver and gold embroideries, worn by Napoleon at his wedding to Marie Louise.
France, 1810.
Musée Napoléon I, Fontainebleau.

Court mantle in silk velvet with embroidery in silk, gold, and silver.
France, ca. 1804.
Museo Napoleonico, Rome.

and roles. In Tuscany, where, after the Medici died out, the dynasty of the Hapsburg Lorraines reigned, the pages – young servants of the Grand Duke – were the only ones who had the right to wear a gala uniform in bright red velvet, decorated with wide, gold-worked braids[9].

The economic crisis in France at the end of the eighteenth century, the Revolution, and the wars, all led to changes in fashion, which led for love and necessity to a sharp limitation in the use of silk, and thus of the most costly fabric, velvet. The proclamation of the Empire, the spectacular ceremony of Napoleon's coronation, and the restoration of a court ordered by the new Emperor were all part of the propaganda designed to favor a new style of life and the relaunching of France as the uncontested capital of elegance. The long capes with gold embroidery, which the Empress and other ladies wore fastened at the waist, as was recorded for posterity by the finest artists of the time, were unfailingly made of velvet. The

Emperor wore velvet or a velvet mantle for his coronation, for his wedding, and when he posed for official portraits. And, all around him, the civilian uniforms of the highest officials of the court once again were made of embroidered silk velvet[10].

The Enlightenment, followed by the Revolution and the reign of Napoleon over the silk-producing countries, had definitively eradicated the Guilds from Europe, and with them, the obligation to manufacture according to strict codes of law. It became legal, even for luxury products, to mix other fibers with silk, such as cotton, wool, or linen; it was possible to invent new market areas and to create an array of products that were not so much marked by their design as by their textures and types of weaves[11]. The patent for the invention of a way of manufacturing a velvet made, not with a supplementary warp, but by cutting floats of weft, was issued in France in 1801; its application to cotton from silk dates from the 1840s,[12] which were certainly the most fertile years in terms of ideas

Jean Auguste Dominique Ingres,
M.me de Senonnes.
Ca. 1813, Musée des Beaux-Arts, Nantes.

Mantle in silk velvet with gold embroidery, worn by Napoleon for his
coronation ceremony in Milan.
France, 1805.
Museo del Risorgimento, Milan.

Man's vest in bombé and chiné velvet.
France, ca. 1850.
Collection of Liana and Carlo Carnevali, Florence.

Detail of the vest shown on page 94.

Cut voided silk velvet with two pile warps, for evening-wear vest.
Lyon, Belleydier, Repiquet et Silvent Manufactory, 1844.
Collection of Thierry Favre, Florence.

"Sans-pareil" velvet.
Lyon, Belleydier, Repiquet et Silvent Manufactory, 1844.
Collection of Thierry Favre, Florence.

Gandin velvet with liseré and pattern wefts for men's vests.
Lyon, Belleydier, Repiquet et Silvent Manufactory, 1844.
Collection of Thierry Favre, Florence.

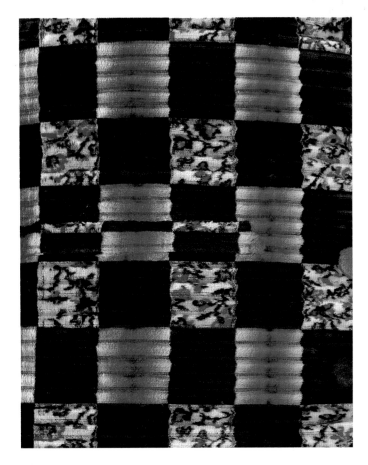

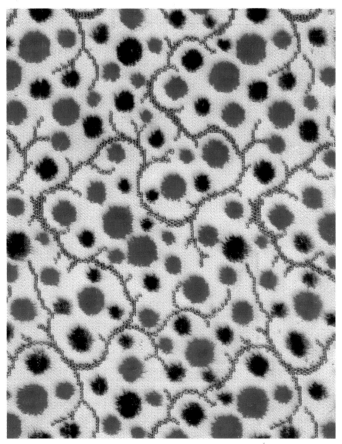

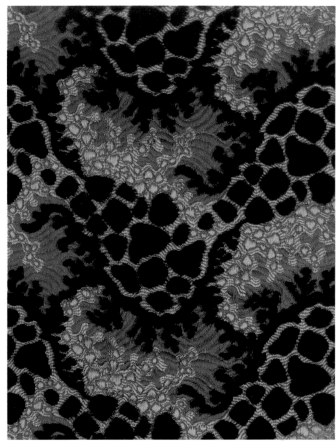

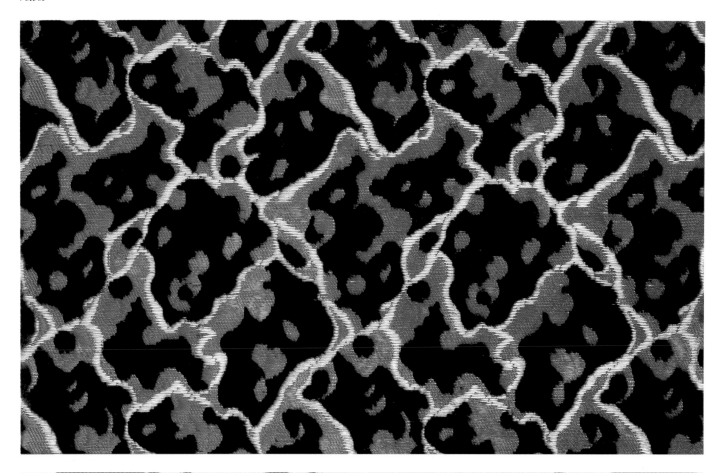

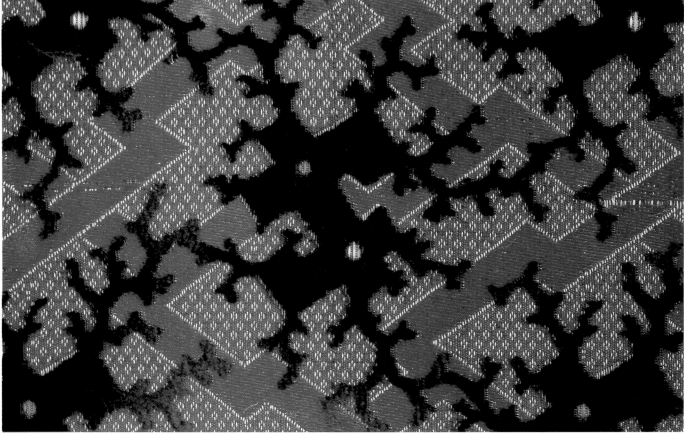

and inventions in the field of textiles. In this sort of velvet, the cutting of the pile was done with a blade out of the loom. With weft floats of different lengths arranged progressively, the final effect was that of corduroy, so well known to us. Because of their durability, cotton velvets, especially cotton corduroys, were the fabrics used predominantly in casual wear; and in this form they have maintained a place of their own in men's wardrobes, which toward the turn of the twentieth century became opaque, austere, and colorless. For men, silk velvet remained in use only for uniforms for special occasions, with a retro cut and style; banished from the more elegant and important articles of clothing, it was relegated to the manufacture of vests and the more refined dressing gowns.

In the manufacture of these specific articles of clothing – one (vests) worn in a discreet position, the other (dressing gowns) used within the walls of the home – general customs permitted, in the nineteenth century, the use of a material that was more sensuous, both to the touch, and in terms of ornamentation and color. In the increasingly specialized differentiation of textile manufacturing, velvets for waistcoats constituted a well defined genre, the pride of a few solidly established companies. The elegance of an article of clothing, which was the only factor that indicated, in a type of apparel that had a strongly unified appearance, the personal tastes and the color preferences of the individual, required the extremely skilled manual labor of a craftsman as well as the division into different types and colors for day wear and evening wear, summer wear and winter wear[13]. Unlike the silks that were intended for female consumers, in which the floral element remained the preferred central theme, the motifs and patterns found in men's waistcoats often appeared to be free to take the form of pure graphic shapes and designs, unconstricted by any or all naturalistic references. And these innovations in terms of design found correspondences in a series of technical inventions and new effects in the history of velvet, perfected during the Forties of the nineteenth century: a binding system had been found which would keep the uncut and cut pile at the same height (sans pareil velvets); another system had been developed to weave figured ground and figured pile together (Gandin velvets); "bombé" velvets were woven with rods of different heights[14]; and lastly, the pile threads in the reverse of the cloth were cut, having been left untied for this purpose in the areas where they were not required by the pattern, in order to keep the fabric as light as possible. The latter system, which made it possible to associate velvet effects with an extremely light fabric, made it possible to use velvet in months other than those in the heart of winter; it was therefore used widely in the finer fabrics used in women's clothing from the Fifties on.

The types of velvets that were brought to the European market by the factories of Lyon were, in the middle of the nineteenth century, astounding in number and were described and listed in the most famous technical manual of those years, the "Dictionnaire des Tissus" by Bezon, mentioned above. Velvets were manufactured with a shot effect in two different hues[15]; velvets and plushes were made with elasticized warps, with silver pile, with ground weave in cashmere, straw, braid, elastic, and ribbon. It would seem that there was no end to the inventions in products "pour modes"; manufacturers of plush, which had regained great favor, especially for men's and women's hats, but also for all sorts of trim, had found methods for imitating different sorts of furs – from astrakhan and otter to chinchilla – with piles of different lengths and curlings.

International expositions, from the 1840s to the 1860s, bore witness to the incredible and vigorous expansion of the silk industry

Men's vest in pile on pile velvet with a plush effect.
France, 1840-1850.
Galleria del Costume, Florence.

Two *Gandin* velvets with liseré effects for men's vests.
Lyon, Belleydier, Repiquet et Silvent Manufactory, 1844.
Collection of Thierry Favre, Florence.

Shawl (detail) in solid cut and uncut
velvet with the warp ends in the rainbow colors.
France, 1810-1820.
Museo del Tessuto e del Costume Storico, Spoleto.

Sample of woven to shape velvet
for women's gowns and borders.
Lyon, Schulz Collection, 1858-1859.
Musée Historique des Tissus, Lyon.

Emile Pingat, Jacket in plain velvet, ca. 1892.
The Brooklyn Museum, New York.

Woven to shape velvet with two
pile warps for shawl.
Lyon, Schulz Collection, 1859-1861.
Musée Historique des Tissus, Lyon.

Ball gown in *au sabre* velvet.
France, Maison Charles Frederick Worth, ca. 1902.
Galleria del Costume, Florence.

Woman's dress in solid silk velvet.
Italy, ca. 1900.
Galleria del Costume, Florence.

of Lyon, which dominated the market and introduced all the fashions, which were immediately propagated by trade publications. Silk continued to be sold at reasonable prices throughout these years, and it spread to the middle class as well, especially when sold through the new commercial system of department stores: a few extremely refined varieties were still restricted to the upper classes, however. The most prestigious fabrics were those with patterns – a version which reappeared after a century, but this time for women's clothing – designed for specific items of clothing, such as mantels and enormous skirts held up by crinoline. For these uses, patterns were designed which fit the flounces nicely, with velvet effects that imitated fringe at the hems, or trompe-l'oeil designs that suggested the presence of two skirts, one draped over the other. The type of velvet with the pile cut on the reverse left the fabric with all the lightness needed to swell up, to the point of forming excessively bell-shaped gowns[16].

The production of such costly fabrics lasted only a few years, because of the serious financial crisis that hit the entire silk industry around 1860; a disease struck the silkworms, and the important American market shut down during the Civil War. Figured velvet disappeared from women's fashion, and since it became necessary to use fabrics of lesser quality, a great deal of work was devoted to the invention of new shapes and new cuts of clothing. Velvet began to reappear in fashion, timidly at first, and then with increasing vigor, from the end of the 1870s onward, with powerful support from the new dictators of women's fashion, the leading Parisian dressmakers – Worth first and foremost among them. From then on, with the return of handsome fabrics at affordable prices to the market, the lines of women's clothing became simpler and simpler: the disappearance of drapery on the skirts invited the admiration of printed and figured patterns and designs. By the end of the century, velvet had won a new and prominent place in women's clothing, both in fashionable dresses, and in the "artistic" ones, as they were called, that had simple and flowing lines, and which were designed by artists and intellectuals[17]. The mechanical production of solid double velvets at reasonable prices allowed the market to make widespread use of this type of fabric, which had in the past always been restricted to the wealthier classes.

Silk velvet, during those years, reached a level of lightness and softness that had never been attained previously, thanks to the production on a very light base of crêpe, the great innovation of the 1890s. Crêpe fabrics, ranging from the impalpable chiffon to the heavier crêpe marocain, quickly became dominant fabrics on the market and in women's wardrobes of the time, attaining their greatest level of popularity in the Twenties. Wide use was made of chiffon velvets, plain and figured; in order to maintain the transparency and lightness of the underlying fabric, the technique of not cutting but yanking away the threads between one motif and the next was employed. The yanking takes off even the last tuft of pile around the pattern, leaving it with sharp and well-defined contours. And what resulted was a fabric that was in part transparent and in part covered, ideal for the interpretation of the ambiguous charm of the femme fatale and of the uninhibited women of the Roaring Twenties, who chose it for the most prestigious and elegant dresses of their wardrobes. The introduction of mechanization in the manufacturing process gave a new range of appearances to velvet, and as a result, made it suitable for new uses: in wool, with a short and soft pile, it became perfect for mantels for daytime use and for the construction of tailleurs, the new item of clothing that perhaps best represented the image of the modern and active woman.

Two photographs by Mariano Fortuny y Madrazo.
Model wearing burnoose made of printed velvet, ca. 1919.
Museo Fortuny, Venice.

On page 102:
Figured ciselé three pile velvet.
Lyon, Bérard et Poucet Manufactory, 1861.
Musée Historique des Tissus, Lyon.

Silk ciselé velvet with four pile warps,
presented at the Paris Exposition of 1900.
Lyon, Poucet Père et Fils Manufactory, 1900.
Musée Historique des Tissus, Lyon.

Woman's dress made of printed solid velvet with Renaissance design.
Venice, Mariano Fortuny y Madrazo, 1910-1915.
Museo Fortuny, Venice.

Printed velvet with Renaissance design.
Venice, Mariano Fortuny y Madrazo,
first quarter of the twentieth century.
Museo Fortuny, Venice.

Printed solid velvet with Turkish design.
Rome, Maria Monaci Gallenga, ca. 1920.
Museo Fortuny, Venice.

Paul Poiret, afternoon dress,
"tout de suite" model, detail, 1919.
Collection Union Franaise des Arts du Costume.

On page 107:
Madeleine Vionnet, evening gown in violet
velvet with floral patterns, 1937-1938.
Collection Union Franaise des Arts du Costume.

Paul Poiret, evening cape, detail of golden thread
embroidery upon velvet, sleeve bordered with fur 1920.

Collection Union Franaise des Arts du Costume.

Paul Poiret, *"fils du ciel"* model, outfit in silk velvet,
lined on the sides and at the neck by a strip of
black satin and gold embroidery, 1923.
Collection Union Franaise des Arts du Costume.

The refined esthetes of the Belle Epoque were certainly not indifferent to the shimmering appearance and sensual texture of velvet, and the fabric became an evocative medium for imaginary worlds of luxury and perversion[18]. Mariano Fortuny, enthralled by their arcane splendor, chose to print the motifs borrowed from the original fabrics in his father's collection of velvet. The techniques which this artist, Venetian by adoption, used to print on his fabrics, often in gold on backgrounds with colors inspired by the city built on a lagoon, are still largely unknown. In perfect line with the fashions of the Renaissance revival which so characterized those years in Italy, he developed designs taken from the sumptuous fifteenth- and sixteenth-century fabrics in his father's collection, and he succeeded in reproducing the light effect of "allucciolato" and the plastic effect

Printed velvet on design by Gino Sensani.
Rome, Maria Monaci Gallenga, ca. 1925.
Private collection, Florence.

of gold wefts. His fabrics and models, with cuts and lines taken from the classics, rapidly won international fame.

Manual printing on fabrics in order to create unique articles, both in clothing and in interior decorating and furnishing, was one of the most exclusive fashions of the first two decades of this century. The artists who applied this technique often made use of velvet, and foremost among them was Maria Monaci Gallenga. Her creations enjoyed enormous success in America, as well as in Europe. She became famous for her design of nuanced patterns using metallic pigments, which left the silks that she used extremely soft and washable. Gallenga designed the clothes as well as the fabric motifs that were to adorn those outfits, preferring the combination of black and gold, typical for that matter of the tastes of those years. By virtue of a clever system that she developed herself, of assembling and breaking down her printing blocks, each garment became in this way personal and exclusive. The designs were suggested by the

Italian tradition of textiles, as was the case with Fortuny; but inspiration also came from artists of the time, who were Gallenga's friends and fellow workers, as committed as she was to the renewal of the design of all crafts products[19].

The Twenties were particularly fertile years, due to the successful collaboration among artists, manufacturers, tailors and dressmakers. And it was thanks to this collaboration that textiles design completely renewed its repertory of ornamentation. The system that was preferred for the decoration of the fabric surfaces was printing, carried out on an industrial basis. The new fashions were always prompted by the best French manufacturers, who were in the vanguard in precisely this sort of production. Those manufacturers employed as designers famed artists, such as Dufy, Ducharne, and Benedictus. In Italy too, thanks to a few industrialists in the area around Como, such as Ravasi, Persicalli, Velca, and Piatti, manufacturing began to take on aspects that went beyond technical production, and to attain the status of design. The cultural debate in question focused on the theme of renewal and singling out a style that could be considered both Italian and modern, and the perfection of manufacturing systems that did not reject tradition, but which could succeed in outdoing it. Velvet, which had played such an important role in Italy's economic and artistic history, went in search of new formulas, with the testing of new esthetic and commercial potential with the use of recently developed artificial fibers.[20] In practical terms, there was no type or design of velvets from the past that the more intelligent of manufacturers did not attempt to reproduce with the use of the newest technology, prompted by the need to renew continuously the sample ranges in consideration of new fashions and the possibility, not really all that remote, of winning new market sectors that had for centuries been the province of the French fashion industry.

With respect to previous historical periods, the twentieth century was to furnish an image of velvet that was far more varied than ever before, well suited to different and versatile possibilities. Velvet was used in its traditional role as a prestige fabric, reserved to the most exclusive creations of high fashion, but it was also used in alternative formulas – suffice it to think of synthetic furs – which made it a sporting and democratic fabric, well suited to all times of the day and all occasions.

Wool velour tailleur used
in Luchino Visconti's film, *Death in Venice*.
Italy, ca. 1915.
Galleria del Costume, Florence.

Women's shoes made of printed velvet.
Venice, Mariano Fortuny y Madrazo Manufactory, ca. 1925.
Museo Fortuny, Venice.

Notes

[1]. More delicate to produce than cut solid velvets. M. Bezon, *op. cit.*, vol. II, 1859, pg. 95.

[2]. For an interpretation of the "a mazze" motif, see F. Podreider, *Storia dei tessuti d'arte in Italia*, Bergamo, 1928, pgg. 224-225.

[3]. Concerning the contemporary definition of the design as "mandorla", see *I principi bambini. Abbigliamento e infanzia nel Seicento*, edited by K. Aschengreen Piacenti, R. Orsi Landini, Florence, 1985, file no. 5.

[4]. At the turn of the century, shades and combinations of colors appeared in fabrics that were entirely new.

[5]. *I principi bambini*, *op. cit.*, file no. 5.

[6]. For a brief history of plushes, see M. Bezon, op. cit., 1859, pgg. 272-274. According to this author, plushes, one must suppose as solid pile fabrics, were first woven in France at the end of the seventeenth century.

[7]. One can find linen plushes, with the pile face turned inward, in the rear of men's undergarments in the eighteenth century.

Silk figured velvets for clothing. Fifties.
Redaelli Velluti Collection.

Colored figured velvets, Fifties.
Redaelli Velluti Collection.

[8]. For miniature velvets, see M. Bezon, *op. cit.*, 1853, pgg. 63 and 81.

[9]. *Lo splendore di una regia corte*, 1983, file no. 9 a, b, c, and no. 10. Concerning civilian uniforms, *I fasti della burocrazia*, edited by M. Cataldi Gallo, C. Cavelli Traverso, E. Coppola, Genoa, 1984, with accompanying bibliography.

[10]. Concerning fashion in the Revolutionary and Napoleonic period, see *Modes and Revolutions, 1780-1804*, exhibition catalogue, New York, 1989 and *The Age of Napoleon*, Paris, exhibition catalogue, New York, 1989.

[11]. Concerning the relationship between the cut and shape of dresses and the types of fabrics employed in the eighteenth and nineteenth centuries, see R. Orsi Landini, *Materia e forma: tessuti e fogge del vestire femminile nei secoli XVIII e XIX*, in *La Galleria del costume 4*, edited by Kirsten Aschengreen Piacenti, Florence, 1990, pgg. 11-21, with accompanying bibliography.

[12]. M. Bezon, op. cit., vol. II, 1859, pgg. 223-226 and pgg. 231-243, concerning cotton velvet, velveteen, and corduroy.

[13]. Concerning this particular range of production, see R. Orsi Landini, *Velluti per gilets nella collezione di Thierry Fauvre di Firenze*, in *Arte Tessile*, no. 2, February 1991, pgg. 48-54.

[14]. M. Bezon, *op. cit.*, 1859, describes many types of *sans pareil* velvets; vol. II, pgg. 54, 58-59; vol. IV, pg. 142. For *Gandin* velvets, vol. IV, pg. 90. For *bombé* velvets, vol. IV, pgg. 141, 295, 299-300. From the descriptions of the same work are taken the typologies treated subsequently as well.

[15]. They are called *Caméléon* velvets: M. Bezon, op. cit., vol. II, 1859, pg. 117.

[16]. R. Orsi Landini, *op. cit.*, 1990, pgg. 17 and foll., for subsequent information as well.

[17]. G. e R. Fanelli, *op. cit.*, 1976, pgg 90-91.

[18]. Everybody knows the passion of Gabriele D'Annunzio for the fabrics, especially the gold brocades and handmade velvets woven by his friend Giuseppe Lisio.

[19]. Concerning Gallenga and his relationships with the contemporary artists, R. Orsi Landini: *L'Artista e il sarto. I rapporti tra arte e moda nell'Italia degli Anni Venti*, in *Anni Venti, La nascita dell'abito moderno*, Florence, 1991, pgg. 46-61.

[20]. Concerning the manufacture of the new articifial synthetic fibers, M. Garofoli, 1991.

Bibliography

1851
Douet d'Arcq, *Comptes de l'Argenterie des Rois de France au XIVe Siècle*, Paris.

1859
M. Bezon, *Dictionnaire général des tissus anciens et modernes*, Lyon, ed. Th. Lepagnez, second edition, voll. II, III, IV.

1868
Girolamo Gargiolli, *L'Arte della Seta in Firenze. Trattato del secolo XV*, Florence, G. Barbera.

1881
G. Marcotti, *Un mercante fiorentino e la sua famiglia*, Florence.

1899
G. Biagi, *Due corredi nuziali fiorentini 1320-1423*, Florence.

1905
P. Molmenti, *La storia di Venezia nella vita privata dalle origini alla caduta della Repubblica*, Bergamo, voll. II; IV edition.

1907
I. Del Lungo, *Women of Florence*, London.

1912
G. Bistort, *Il magistrato delle pompe nella Repubblica di Venezia*, Bologna.

1915
E. Pandiani, *Vita privata genovese del Rinascimento*, Genoa.

1927
L. Brenni, *I velluti di seta italiani*, Milan.
A. Mancini, U. Dorini, E. Lazzareschi, *Statuto della corte dei mercanti in Lucca del MCCCLXXVI*, Florence.

1928
L. Frati, *La vita privata in Bologna dal secolo XIII al XVII*, Bologna, second edition.
Fanny Podreider, *Storia dei tessuti d'arte in Italia*, Bergamo.

1964-1969
R. Levi Pisetzsky, *Storia del costume in Italia*, vol. V, Milan.

1966
F. Edler De Roover, *Andrea Banchi Florentine Silk Manufacturer and Merchant in the Fifteenth Century*, in *Studies in Medieval and Renaissance History*, vol. III, Lincoln, pgg. 221-285.

1974
D. Devoti, *L'arte del tessuto in Europa*, Milan.

1976
G. and R. Fanelli, *Il tessuto moderno Disegno Moda Architettura 1890-1940*, Florence.
R. Morelli, *La seta fiorentina nel Cinquecento*, Milan.

1980
J. Coural: *Paris, Mobilier National. Soieries Empire. Inventaire des collections publiques françaises*. Paris.

1981

E. Bazzani, *Velluti di Seta*, in Donata Devoti - Giovanni Romano (edited by), *Tessuti antichi nelle chiese di Arona*, Turin, pgg. 81-118.

R. Bonito Fanelli, *Five Centuries of Italian Textiles: 1300-1800*, Florence.

R. Bonito Fanelli and P. Peri, *Tessuti italiani del Rinascimento*, exhibition catalogue, Florence.

P. Massa, *La "Fabbrica" dei velluti genovesi da Genova a Zoagli*, Genoa.

P. Peri, *Il parato di Niccolò V*, Florence.

M. Praz, *La filosofia dell'arredamento*, Milan.

1983

Lo splendore di una regia corte. Uniformi e livree del Granducato di Toscana 1765-1799, edited by R. Orsi Landini, L. Ragusi, exhibition catalogue, Florence.

L. Monnas, *The Vestments of Sixtus IV at Padua*, in *Bulletin de Liaison du Centre International d'Etude des Textiles Anciens*, no. 57-58, pgg. 104-105.

Tessuti serici italiani 1450-1530, edited by Chiara Buss, Grazietta Butazzi, Marina Molinelli, exhibition catalogue, Milan.

1984

Fasti della burocrazia. Uniformi civili e di corte dei secoli XVIII-XIX, edited by Marzia Cataldi Gallo, Carla Cavelli Traverso, Elisa Coppola, exhibition catalogue, Genoa.

L. Portoghesi, *Per una storia del costume nel Seicento umbro*, in *Il costume e l'immagine pittorica nel Seicento umbro*, catalogue of the exhibition at Foligno, Florence.

P. Thornton, *Il gusto della casa: storia per immagini dell'arredamento 1620-1920*, Milan.

1985

R. De Gennaro, *Velluti operati del secolo XV col motivo delle 'gricce' 1*, Florence.

I principi bambini. Abbigliamento e infanzia nel Seicento, edited by K. Aschengreen Piacenti, R. Orsi Landini, exhibition catalogue, Florence.

1986

I. Chiappini di Sorio, *Le premesse storiche della tessitura a Venezia*, in *Origine e sviluppo dei velluti a Venezia: il velluto allucciolato d'oro*, Venice, pgg. 9-13.

G. and R. Fanelli, *Il tessuto Art Deco e Anni Trenta*, Florence.

L. Monnas, *Developments in Figured Velvet Weaving in Italy During the 14th Century*, in *Bulletin de Liaison du Centre International d'Etude des Textiles Anciens*, no. 63-64, I-II, pgg. 63-100.

1987

R. De Gennaro, *Velluti operati del XV secolo col motivo "de'camini"*, Florence.

L. Monnas, *The Vestments of Henry VII at Stonyhurst*, in *Bulletin de Liaison du Centre International d'Etude des Textiles Anciens*, no. 65, 1987, pgg. 69-80.

M. R. Montiani Bensi, *La produzione della manifattura genovese Ardizzoni*, in *Le tappezzerie nelle dimore storiche. Studi e metodi di conservazione*, Proceedings of the conference of Florence, Turin, pgg. 101-111.

A. Argentieri Zanetti, *Dizionario tecnico della tessitura*, Udine.

1988

R. Berveglieri, *L'Arte dei Tintori e il nero di Venezia*, in *I mestieri della moda a Venezia dal XIII al XVIII secolo*, exhibition catalogue, Venice, pgg. 55-61.

F.W. Carter, *Cracow's Transit Textile Trade 1390-1795: a Geographical Assessment*, in *Textile History*, vol. XIX, no. 1, pgg. 23-60.

Le sete impero dei palazzi napoleonici, exhibition catalogue, Florence.

I mestieri della moda a Venezia dal XIII al XVIII secolo, exhibition catalogue, Venice.

R. Orsi Landini, *I paramenti sacri della cappella palatina di Palazzo Pitti*, Florence.

1989

A.A.V.V., *Le Vêtement: Histoire, archéologie, et symbolique vestimentaires au Moyen Age*, Paris.

Arti del Medio Evo e del Rinascimento Omaggio ai Carrand 1889, edited by Giovanna Gaeta Bertelà and Beatrice Paolozzi Strozzi, exhibition catalogue, Florence.

C. de Merindol, *Signes de hierarchie sociale à la fin du Moyen Age d'après le vêtement. Méthodes et Recherches*, in A.A.V.V., *Le Vêtement.*, op. cit., Paris.

D. Devoti, *La Seta. Tesori di un'antica arte lucchese*, Lucca.

Modes and Revolutions 1780-1804, exhibition catalogue, Paris.

L. Monnas, *Silk Cloths Purchased for the Great Wardrobe of the Kings of England*, in *Textile History*, vol. XX, no. 2, pgg. 283-320.

D. Roche, *La culture des apparences: Une histoire du vêtement XVIIe-XVIIIe Siècle*, Paris.

The Age of Napoleon - Costume from Revolution to Empire: 1789-1815, exhibition catalogue, New York.

1990

Mobili soffici, edited by A. Zanni, Milan.

R. Orsi Landini, *Materia e forma: tessuti e fogge del vestire femminile nei secoli XVIII e XIX*, in *La Galleria del costume 4*, edited by Kirsten Aschengreen Piacenti, Florence, pgg. 11-21.

1991

F. Cardini, *I Re Magi di Benozzo Gozzoli*, Florence.

C. Ghiara, *La tintura nera genovese: "La migliore di quante se ne facesse al mondo"*, in *Seta a Genova 1491-1991*, edited by Piera Rum, exhibition catalogue, Genoa, pgg. 22-28.

R. Orsi Landini, *L'Artista e il sarto. I rapporti fra arte e moda nell'Italia degli Anni Venti*, in *Anni Venti La nascita dell'abito moderno*, edited by Aurora Fiorentini, Roberta Orsi Landini and Stefania Ricci, exhibition catalogue, Florence, pgg. 35-63.

R. Orsi Landini, *Velluti per gilets dalla collezione di Thierry Favre di Firenze*, in *Arte Tessile*, no. 2, February 1991, pgg. 48-54.

M. Garofoli, *Le Fibre intelligenti. Un secolo di storia e cinquanta anni di moda*, Milan.

1992

R. Bonito Fanelli, *Il motivo della melagrana nei tessuti italiani al tempo di Piero della Francesca*, in *Tessuti italiani al tempo di Piero della Francesca*, without indication of printing, (Petruzzi Editore), pgg. 36-43.

O. Morelli, *Prime riflessioni intorno alla regola del "porre" e del "levare"*, in *Tessuti italiani al tempo di Piero della Francesca*, op. cit., pgg. 80-82.

R. Orsi Landini, *Le sete francesi del periodo neoclassico e impero. Prodotto e immagine*, in *Il tessuto nell'età del Canova*, edited by Marta Cuoghi Costantini, Milan, pgg. 15-33

F. Piponnier, *Emplois et diffusion de la soie en France à la fin du Moyen Age*, report delivered at the conference "La Seta in Europa: Secc. XIII-XX", Prato, 4-9 May 1992.

R. Schorta, *Il trattato dell'Arte della Seta. A Florentine 15th Century Treatise on Silk Manufacturing*, in *Bulletin du CIETA* no. 69, pgg. 57-86.

1993

Moda alla Corte dei Medici. Gli abiti di Cosimo, Eleonora, don Garzia restaurati, edited by Cristina Piacenti, exhibition catalogue, Florence.

Without a date.

D. Davanzo Poli, *I mestieri della moda a Venezia nei sec. XIII-XVIII. Documenti*, Venice.

L. Bardini Barbafiera, *Elementi di tecnica tessile*, Milan, V edition.

Gianfranco Ferré, trousers in silk velvet.
Fall-winter collection 1992-1993.
Photograph by Gian Paolo Barbieri.

VELVET IN FASHION
From the Thirties to the Present

Aurora Fiorentini Capitani - Stefania Ricci

In the history of fashion, velvet has never really gone out of style or disappeared from the market. At an unflagging pace, interrupted only now and again, and then only briefly, it has succeeded in maintaining intact its aristocratic allure, both in the corduroy version used in casual wear, and in the smooth and printed versions of more elegant clothing.

The reason for this success lies in the intrinsic qualities of this fabric. Warm, soft, and dense, pleasant to wear and to touch, versatile in its infinite array of applications in the sportiest and the most elegant articles, velvet is flexible but substantial, and it maintains the rigor of a line while still inducing a state of exaltation, with the reverberation of its reflections and colors, producing chromatic effects of remarkable beauty.

The centuries-long tradition of a fabric that has always been considered lavish and prestigious is, moreover, a seal of quality, which establishes velvet as a classic fabric, particularly popular in times of shifting directions and of a return to the more traditional values of femininity and elegance.

During the Thirties, in fact, after a decade of prints and laminated fabrics, there was a general rediscovery of the venerable and evocative qualities of velvet, which immediately enjoyed a very fertile revival. French dressmakers, who were then dictating law in international fashion and style, began to include in their collections full-length evening gowns in smooth or printed velvet, with velvet accessories and trim on the collars, cuffs, and lapels, thus conferring a precious and refined touch to daytime wear.

The Great Depression that began with the Crash of 1929 had heavily marked the end of the Roaring Twenties, and with the disappearance of that decade, came the elimination of a certain type of woman, the garconne, distinguished by her androgynous body, her ambiguous sexuality, her short cropped hair, knee length skirts, and the tubular lines of her outfits. With the dawn of the new decade, therefore, a need was felt to return to a more conventional feminine image, soft and sensual, underscored by a type of clothing that revealed a bust with some substance – as opposed to the flat chests of the previous decade – a waist where nature put it, a flaired skirt, and an ankle-length hemline.

The introduction of the bias cut, the product of the inventive vision of Madeleine Vionnet, maintained narrow waist and hips, made it easier for women to walk, and allowed a swaying and sensuous gait typical of the femme fatale, a type that was propagated around the world on the silver screen. The dresses worn by American movie stars had a major influence on both high fashion and on dress makers in the small towns of the entire world, with the cunning balance midway between the clinging lines and the "pruderie" of the clothing, which uncovered and yet concealed, revealing a nude back while still covering the bust with the modesty of a nun's habit.

An endless source of inspiration was the blue velvet dress worn by Greta Garbo in a number of scenes in the film Ispiration, in which the divine Garbo played Yvonne Valbert, the muse of the Latin Quarter. The same can be said of Joan Crawford's little velvet bolero jackets and her transformable black chiffon velvet outfits, for afternoon or evening wear. Crawford's clothing clung to her body, and loosened from the knees down in an array of dense godets[1]. With their way of catching and reflecting light, plain satins and velvets exalted the movements of the body and the classic cadences of drapery. Better than any other fabric, they underscored the plastic qualities of an outfit and the complex tailoring and construction, imposed by high fashion, after the years of simplicity that had

Madeleine Vionnet, evening gown with draped top and ample skirt in purple velvet, 1938-1939. Collection Union Franaise des Arts du Costume.

Evening gowns in silk velvet, Sartoria Zecca, 1933-1935. Galleria del Costume di Palazzo Pitti. Donazione Umberto Tirelli, Florence.

Lucien Lelong, evening gown made of black silk velvet,
Vogue, October 1934.

Mainbocher, evening gown made of velvet printed with white flowers.
Excelsior Modes, 1934.

Atelier Worth, Sheilah Hennessy
with a black velvet outfit.
Photograph by George Hoyningen-Huene,
Excelsior Modes, 1934.

Sheer velvet eveing gown, *Excelsior Modes.*

Advertising page for "Intact Velvet",
Vogue, October 1934.

On page 121:
Balenciaga, detail of an outfit in caramel-colored velvet,
displayed in Lyon in 1985,
for the Balenciaga retrospective, Musée Galliera.

Balenciaga, purple theatrical costume for Alice Cocéa, inspired by the Spanish
Renaissance for "Echee à Don Juan", Theatre des Ambassadeurs.

facilitated the degree to which patterns could be reproduced.

In the winter of 1932, velvet triumphed in the creations of every French couturier, from Paquin and Lanvin to Chanel and Mainbocher. In combination with other textiles, such as silk and wool, in jackets, mantles, and outfits, velvet became the star fabric of evening wear[2]. The French textiles manufacturers, in turn, promoted this fashion trend by keeping the level of quality of their production exceedingly high. The "Nabab" velvets by Chatillon Mouly Roussel and the "Nocturne", "Tahiti", "Morocco", and "Mameluck" velvets by Ducharne – with their exotic and seductive names – were distinguished by their rich deep colors. Bianchini-Férier launched the "Camea" velvet, which was as smooth and shiny as satin, and the "piqué Granité". Coudurier's "Paysan" presented a finely gauffrered surface, while the "Bagheera" velvet by Coudurier Fructus Descher was the true discovery of the season; it was opaque and elastic, perfect for all sorts of drapery, and incredibly light.

In an effort to create a model of inimitable refinement, high fashion moved during the Thirties in two different directions, which clashed only in appearance. On the one hand, high fashion promoted costly simplicity, made up of precious fabrics and ingenious details; on the other hand there was an unstoppable flow of prints and patterns, feeding upon continual historical references.

In 1937, Molyneux dedicated an entire collection to the Middle Ages, creating velvet evening gowns with great wing sleeves and copious hoods, trimmed with fur. It was, however, Elsa Schiaparelli above all others who was responsible for the greatest innovations of these years.
This designer/dressmaker of Italian origin adopted "volants" and "ruches" in the most elegant and sumptuous outfits, with embroideries on tight-fitting jackets not unlike corsets, borrowed from the fashions of 1860 to 1880[3].

It is clear that velvet was equally important in each of the two trends. It had always been a costly fabric, and it was thus capable of adding value to even the simplest outfit, with its illustrious history that featured in the last decades of the nineteenth century – the time to which the fashion of the thirties made reference – one of its most successful periods.

Despite the excellent results achieved by French haute couture in maintaining production at the levels of the previous decade, the great Wall Street Crash of 1929 had slowed the growth of the textiles industry, especially the manufacturers of cotton and silk, with a resulting emphasis on artificial and synthetic fibers, which had first begun to make their appearance in the first decade of the century. Their spread throughout the Thirties cannot be explained solely by the overall economic depression that was so badly affecting more traditional fabrics. Rather one must look to the atmosphere of experimentation that was sweeping through the world of fashion, through the direct influence of such artists as Cocteau and Dalì, close collaborators with Schiaparelli and Chanel. In this climate of invention and modernity, acetates and rayon invaded the market and were turned into velvets, crepes, and satins, with unbelievably popular prices and unexpected potential[4].

In Italy, the market sector of "new textiles" encountered a particularly favorable atmosphere for development and growth, bound up with the dire straits in which the Italian textiles industry found itself as a result of competition and the hostile foreign policy adopted by the government. When WWI broke out, Italy had been in fourth place in the world rankings for the production of artificial and synthetic fibers, the leading fibers in the category being rayon and flock. The Snia Viscosa company, which was founded in Turin in

Battilocchi, evening gown in black velvet
with tulle appliques, in *Tessili Nuovi*,
summer 1949.

Balmain, gown in rayon velvet with a
wreath-shaped corset, filled with flowers,
in *Tessili Nuovi*, fall 1949.

Page of advertising for special types of
finish by Arnold Hoffman, in *Tessili
Nuovi*, summer 1949.

1916, became the largest manufacturer of new fibers, not only in Italy but in all of Europe, and in 1939 the company also took control of the Cisa-Viscosa group[5].

After 1935, in the wake of the economic sanctions imposed upon Italy by the League of Nations in retribution for her expansionistic efforts in Ethiopia, Mussolini began to implement his policies in support of the growing production of and reliance upon Italian products. In the area of fashion, the government promoted "vestire italiano", meaning "dress Italian", an effort to eliminate all French influence, while in the field of textiles, the government pushed for both the production of traditional fabrics such as silk, wool, and hemp as well as experimentation with new yarns and fibers.

The types of fabrics that were best suited for the new treatments were those whose processing did not require a great deal of mechanical intervention, which is to say, those without a great deal of figured patterns. They were smooth fabrics, regular and compact with a tight warp/weft, such as *"angel skin"*, satin, and muslin in rayon and silk; *"duvet"*, drap and velvet in flock, "lanital" and wool[6].

The campaign in favor of textile autarchy culminated in a great exposition of Italian textiles, held in the Circus Maximus in Rome between 1937 and 1938, making the triumph of Snia Viscosa and the new textiles, symbols of the future official. Satiny knits, velvets as light as crepes, blends of opaque natural silks and shiny artificial silks, manufactured in an infinite range of colors – all contributed to a considerable enrichment of the traditional repertory of classical fabrics.

The spotlight of popular interest focused upon velvet, because it was considered Italy's national fabric par excellence; Italy had been unrivalled in her production of velvet for many centuries. As early as the mid-Thirties, the Ventura fashion house in Milan, in an effort to develop a purely Italian fashion, free of all French influence, had repeatedly featured domestically manufactured velvet, as an exquisitely Italian fabric, in its collections.

It is no accident therefore that the Roman exhibition should be accompanied by an exhibition of historical Italian velvets, a useful object lesson for the modern manufacturers of the cloth, and an excellent source of inspiration for an artistic vision of designs, that could be adapted to modern requirements[7]. The NIVEA company of Gerenzano (NIVEA stood for Nuova Industria di Velluti e Affini, meaning New Manufacturer of Velvets and Related Products) presented a wrinkle-proof velvet in Rome which was delicate, while still providing durability and beauty. Through a chemical process of condensation, it became possible to preserve the best qualities of velvet, while improving the fabric's properties and value both in tactile and visual terms, with new qualities of water-resistance[8].

Alongside the production of artificial and synthetic fibers, companies such as Celanese and Rhodiatoce carried on experimentation into new printing methods, which made it possible to obtain decorative effects in velvet blends with rayon acetate pile, and ground in rayon viscose, through the finely calibrated destruction of the pile[9]. The creation of the new velvets implied technical problems with the spinning, dyeing, printing, and weaving, and the solution of those problems provided a great variety of new ideas and discoveries which were fundamental to the development of the sector in the period immediately following the war. But first and foremost it completely overturned the traditional values and standards of judgement, and opened the production of these fabrics, previously the prerogative of a restricted elite, to new sectors of the market and to a completely different use in the apparel industry.

Vanna, mantle made of iridescent taffeta on figured velvet, in *Tessili Nuovi*, fall 1948.

Biki, gala evening gown in black velvet with satin trim and fringes in paillettes, in *Tessili Nuovi*, fall 1948.

Velvet

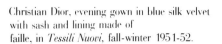

If silk and cotton velvets, which were so fragile and easy to damage, had till now been used exclusively in outfits for special occasions, worn rarely and therefore relatively safe from wear, the production of velvets made of cotton and acetate, which were extremely durable, or nylon, which were washable and wrinkle-proof, or in silk and rayon, which were elastic and soft, opened up an endless array of new uses [10].

The fashion of these years tended to emphasize this new production. The styles that dressmakers already began to favor in the Forties were perfect for the application of new materials, which featured qualities of softness and plasticity, and could be yielding and fall particularly well, thus meeting the requirements of a fairly complex cut and assembly.

The obligatory experimentation imposed by the Second World War continued to yield fruit in the postwar years, triggering in the textiles industry an acclerated process of stylistic and technical experimentation, which went on to affect a growing number of

Biki, pied-de-poule mantle over a purple rayon velvet skirt and a blouse made of purple wool, in *Tessili Nuovi*, winter 1949.

fibers, in part thanks to the enormous recovery of industrial activity. France and – after the spectacular debut of Italian Style in 1951 – Italy, alongside Germany, Switzerland, and England, witnessed a proliferation of companies involved in the design and manufacture of new products, among which were a great many velvets, often made of blends, with increasingly refined effects.

Once again this material, particularly open to all sorts of unusual interpretations and applications, captured the full attention not only of the manufacturers, but also of the designers of France and Italy, in an incessant search for products suited to the changing requirements of lifestyle and tastes. Bianchini-Férier, Chatillon, Ducharne, Hurel, Italviscosa, Rhodiatoce, Textiloses and Textiles, Legler, in a partnership with Belenciaga, Balmain, and Carven and, amongst the Italians, Marucelli, Biki, Veneziani, and Antonelli, all developed remarkable corduroys and figured velvets, rainbow-effect or chenille-effect velvets, and Rhodia organdy velvets which completely revolutionized women's clothing in the space of just a

Veneziani Sport, overblouse for the mountains made of sheer velvet in *Tessili Nuovi*, winter 1951-1952.

...lo chic del velluto è unico e la moda lo riprende in pieno in questa stagione, soprattutto per gli abiti da sera e da cocktail. Il modello è ampio, con gran décolleté trattenato da spalline e ha il bustino guarnito con pizzo macramé d'argento.

Evening gown made of silk velvet with a corset trimmed with macramé lace. Page of advertising for FISAC (Fabbriche Italiane Seterie ed Affini Como - the Italian Manufacturers of Silk and Allied Products, Como) in *Tessili Nuovi*, 1952-1953.

few collections[11].

After the obligatory elimination of all excess elegance imposed by the difficult years of the war, at the end of the Forties, fashion turned extremely feminine once again, proffering an ideal of a very sophisticated woman, whose body was to be more than ever emphasized by lavish, soft, and enveloping fabrics. And it was in these same years that the desire for a life free of all strictures and limitations and comforted by all sorts of luxury found its expression in the mythical "New Look" from Dior. This look clearly demonstrated – in the lines, the materials, especially velour and taffeta, and colors – that there was a general return to the venerable splendors of the Second Empire. The rounded shoulders, the florid bust, the belt pulled tight to emphasize the narrowness of the waistline, ample long skirts, open shoes with narrow high heels all worked to make the female figure intriguing; like never before it seemed indispensable to have fabrics marked by body and substance, along with special properties of sensuality.

Velvet, as early as the first Parisian collections of 1948, in the interpretations by Fath and Lanvin, Madame Grés, and Balenciaga, appeared to be the material that, more than any other, could make the best of these specific requirements, exalting the brilliance of the ranges of color and the softness of the surfaces[12]. Indeed, in the returning economic security and political stability that followed the war, velvet was presented in the better established natural fibers, such as silk and especially cotton, which could be used in outfits for sports and for afternoon wear. As Italy began recovering full industrial activity, companies that specialized in the creation of the more traditional fabrics – such as the Redaelli company, which had been one of the leading manufacturers of high-quality velvet prior to the war – also returned to work. In these years, Redaelli succeeded in producing 60 percent of Italy's velvet, exporting its fabrics chiefly to Paris, for use there by the French couturiers.

And among those couturiers, Dior in particular emphasized the allure and the elegance of velvet, making free use of it in sumptuous articles and in outfits that were definitely quite sporty. In Dior's Ailée line from the fall-winter of 1948-1949, we find velvet to be the unrivalled star, with a midnight blue outfit, entirely embroidered in gold silk yarn – purchased by the Duchess of Windsor – and in the splendid "Minuit" evening cape in black silk, decorated with appliqués of flowers and garlands. In the winter collection of the following year, "Milieu du Siecle", velour appeared once again as the guiding theme, along with satin and faille for cocktail outfits and for evening wear, with such romantic names as "Pisanello" and "Cigno Nero", meaning Black Swan, or else together with twill for morning or afternoon outfits[13]. High fashion at the end of the decade was still the exclusive domain of the French, and it imposed its creative solutions upon the attention of the world; it was imitated everywhere in accordance with the dictates of its authoritative spokesmen. Specific styles benefitted from this situation; so did certain fabrics.

During the optimistic years of European reconstruction, from 1950 onward toward the peaks of the most explicit consumerism, the whirlwind of styles and fabrics became increasingly frantic: for the new seasons, wool, silk, and cotton velvets were blended with experimental fibers or else with the well fabrics – rayon, nylon, and acetate – with continual renewals and renovations, rapid changes in appearance and texture, thus providing the emancipated modern woman a number of diversified practical applications. From the middle of the Fifties onward, in fact, linen or cotton and viscose blends, and silk and acrylic blends, prevailed quite decisively over the qualities of the more traditional velvets. Even a spokesman for

Balmain, grey tailleur with lapel, bows at the neckline, and lining of the cape in grey velvet, in *La Donna*, September 1954.

Jole Veneziani, evening gowns made of white jersey and black silk velvet with silver embroideries, in *Tessili Nuovi*, 1952-1953.

Maria Antonelli, cape made of Rhodia Italia velvet, in *Linea*, winter 1954.

LINEA
AUTUNNO

ANNO XIX · 1954 · N. 62
L. 700
(ABB. ANNUO L. 3500)

I TESSILI NUOVI
LES TEXTILES NOUVEAUX
THE NEW TEXTILES
LOS NUEVOS TEXTILES
DIE NEUEN TEXTILIEN

Capucci, mantle made of ruby-red velvet,
headgear by Clemente Cartoni with heraldic
devices of the noble families of Rome,
cover of *Linea, Tessili Nuovi*, fall 1954.

conservatism in fashion, such as the Maison Dior, the emblem of timeless chic, beginning with the "Obliqua" line in 1951, was to make its way, through a careful study of materials, to the innovative solutions of the celebrated H-lines and A-lines of 1954 and 1955, the forerunners of new minimalist geometrics. In these significant collections, considerable space was devoted to synthetics, among which there stood out a versatile nylon velour, Velvenyl, which immediately proved – with its wrinkle-proof and stretch-proof qualities – that the more classic components of other fabrics were obsolete. With excellent results in terms of prints and figured fabrics and with vast possibilities of application, Velvenyl would allow velvet to spread to a far larger segment of the market, where its functional and modern aspects were sharply preferred to its more exclusive aspects [14].

During the same years, Balenciaga proposed a "velour cannellé" in a Bodin acetate, alongside those made of silk by the manufacturers of Lyon, as a further confirmation that practicality had taken on great importance, even in the most demanding articles of high fashion [15]. Velvet attained all of its potential, especially in the cocktail outfit, the true focal point of fashion in the Fifties, due to its eclectic qualities. In morning garb and dress for the more sporty occasions, the practical and offhand corduroy was preferred, while the details were left to the smoother velvet: small collars, jacket lapels, pocket flaps, and cuffs. For elegant afternoon wear, the cocktail outfit gave smooth and solid-color velvet every opportunity to express itself, playing on the brilliance and the rainbow effects that were best suited to it. Particularly refined effects could be obtained together with other materials, as in the two-piece outfit presented by Jean Patou in 1956, where a bordeaux viscose Marescot velvet was covered by the light mechanically produced lace with a trelliswork effect [16].

During this decade, Italian high fashion showed great interest in those types of velvet that were most promising in terms of elegance and transformability. From 1953 onward, moreover, "Textile Promotion", which debuted on the prestigious runway of Sala Bianca at Palazzo Pitti, in Florence, played the role of reinforcing a partnership, which already existed for that matter, between designers and fabric manufacturers, with the aim of promoting Italian fashion products around the world. The partnerships between Bemberg, Vanna, and Veneziani; between the Cotonoficio Legler, Emilio Pucci, and Capucci; between Italviscosa, Marucelli, and Antonelli; between Scacchi and Carosa all became famous – while Falconetto began to market outfits of remarkable taste and wearability made of his own velvets [17]. Many "historical" companies enjoyed a particular notoriety in this phase – this was certainly true of Fede Cheti, which had long specialized in the manufacture of magnificent printed and figured velvets, present both in the field of apparel and of interior decoration. Another case was that of Redaelli, which supplied Italian designers of the first order, such as Valentino, but also managed to conquer the closed world of Parisian haute-couture, selling velvets on an exclusive basis to Dior, Yves Saint-Laurent, and Givenchy [18].

The runway presentations in Florence also involved men's fashion, which was an absolutely new development, not found in France. Brioni and Litrico, along with Datti and Franzoni, adopted velvet in the smooth version, with decorated borders, for innovative smoking jackets – innovative both in the selection of materials and in the introduction of new colors, such as rust and bordeaux [19]. But the truly new development was "cord" velvet, i.e., corduroy, which joined Prince of Wales and checks in the area of sportswear and daywear, inspired by an image of a revisited English countryside.

Barthet, hats in *La Donna*, March 1955.

Madeleine de Rauch, nylon velvet (velvenyl) outfit, by
Raimon Velours, in *L'Officiel*, September 1954.

Garnett, cocktail outfit made of "Nailon Rhodiatoce"
and black "Rhodia" velvet, classic in cut,
in *Linea Italiana*, 1965-1966.

Tizzoni, perforated and embroidered black velvet cocktail outfit. Yellow interior by Giò Ponti, at the Tenth Triennial of Milan, in *Linea*, winter 1954.

The popularity of these solutions became ever greater in the following decades, thanks to the creation of American myths in the movies, music, and theater, through celebrities such as Paul Newman and Arthur Miller, who worked to spread a casual and non-conformist look.

A specific trend of these years was the return in a modern interpretation of the old worked velvets, which were reminiscent of soft and elaborate multicolored oriental rugs. The palette included a great many greens, reds, all the warm tones; nuances of ochre and browns in the winter; greys and pastel shades in the spring.

In the Renaissance and nineteenth-century atmospheres recreated by the Florentine runway presentations, velvet reigned supreme, giving new value to the simple lines of daywear, either in ample, balloon version or in the close-fitting mermaid version, with a clear emphasis on the elegance of expansive crinolines, mantels and capes; particularly celebrated and still justly remembered were the versions by Carosa and Antonelli. But the references to tradition are to be found only in the names and the lines of the collections, since the materials employed were a distillation of the latest discoveries in the fields of textiles and dyeing.

In the sector of velvets made of cottons or blends, Visconti di Modrone, Pontoglio, and Legler dominate; the latter was a promoter of a great many undertakings at a very high level, and was present in nearly all of the collections of Italian high fashion in the Fifties and Sixties. With such advertising slogans as "si stira da solo il velluto di quest'anno" – meaning "this year's velvet irons itself" – in 1956 or "il velluto è magnifico e niente delicato" – meaning "the velvet is magnificent and not delicate at all" – in 1959, the manufacturer, located in Ponte S. Pietro, introduced a new fabric to the market, "Relax-Legler", a cotton velvet treated with special processes, and which proved to be totally wrinkle-proof: when left hanging for an hour or two, it practically ironed itself. This revolutionary fabric also presented the great advantage of being water-washable even at home, and it was immediately adopted by Biki for the 1956 collection.

The times dominated by beautiful but – unfortunately excessively delicate – velvets, seemed incredibly long ago. In this version, "Relax-Legler", warranted by a special distinctive marking on the selvage, declared itself to be stain-proof too, which is to say, capable of repelling all liquids except grease and alcohol[20]. Wrinkle-proof, crease-proof, and relatively stain-proof, this fabric outdid itself, and was offered in an extensive range of colors, with the most refined of

131

Emilio Pucci, poncho and trousers made of silk velvet,
Sicilian collection, 1955.

Emilio Pucci, chalet Pijamas made of printed velvet,
fall/winter collection 1966.

Emilio Pucci, overblouse made of printed velvet and trousers made of
Emilioform, fall/winter collection 1963.

Emilio Pucci, overblouse made of printed silk velvet and embroidered with
sequins and beads, stretch leggings in orchid-pattern Helanca.
Paggio collection 1966.

Ken Scott, body suit with *"gallant"* design velvet jacket.
Spring collection 1969.

designs, including the paisley-motif prints and fantasy prints with geometric patterns (for instance, the "window-bar" patterns), or floral motifs with such amusing names as "Poker", "Ye' Ye'", and "Soiré".

In France, a stretch velvet was patented, made of "Ileanca" and "Leacril", with excellent qualities of wearability and adherence. Great innovations lay in wait for velvet, however, during the following decades, made in blends with Orlon and Dralon, designed to take on the appearance of Prince of Wales, of which even the two- or three-color designs were recreated, or of Scotch tartans, selected in the most traditional colorways[21]. In the Sixties, there was an explosion of fabrics with large patterns, which was encouraged by the perfection of techniques of production and engraving of the printing plates, so that it now became possible to attain sophisticated nuanced – or "sfumato" – effects. Emilio Pucci and Ken Scott were to base their collections on the frequent use of smooth printed velvets, in cotton, silk, and acrylic, in the most representative graphics and in a daring array of colors, produced by companies such as Redaelli, Visconti di Modrone, and Legler.

These were the years that introduced the hippie culture of the flower children, human and political interest for oppressed ethnic minorities, and of progress in humanity's efforts to reach distant planets: all events that were destined to become trends used by the fashion industry.

Bright and clashing colors, essential and futuristic patterns, references to exotic oriental atmospheres were, in fact, the distinguishing features of the most fashionable fabrics from the mid-Sixties onward. All of the qualities of velvet attained an extremely soft texture, becoming soft and silky, and providing the greatest levels of comfort. Methods of processing and finishing multiplied, ranging from the very fine cord that made them more flexible, to smooth solid velvet or patterned pile, in shiny, opaque, and iridiscent versions[22]. Amomg the "imprimé", especially those selected by Balmain, Valentino, Saint Laurent, and Capucci, enormous success was enjoyed by the extended floral patterns, used for evening wear in a "lamé" version, either embroidered or flocked. Between 1965 and 1970, Abraham and Ducharne created several of these on an exclusive basis for Givenchy, playing skillfully with effects of relief and "moiré", succeeding in the simulation of the iridescent effects of cellophane or the nap of certain priceless furs[23]. Among the geometric motifs, particular acclaim greeted the presentation of stripes (including the optical versions) and the multi-colored checks, which had to be based on a light and bright background. These were used widely by Courrèges, Cardin, Rabanne, Marucelli, and De Barentzen, to create pied-de-poules and Scotch tartans with cunningly designed polychrome effects. Crushed velvets were also rediscovered, in the Lastex version, providing imitations of improbable furs, such as Breitschwanz, in pastel shade, and as early as 1953 and 1954, Marucelli – in conjunction with Nivea of Gerenzano – used them for some remarkable articles of evening wear[24].

Elasticized velvets, like those marketed by Cosserat and Charles Etiènne, moreover, were to find extensive use in the sportswear lines of the leading houses of high and boutique fashion, fitting perfectly into the manufacture of leggings and coats for mountaineering and for leisure time. Designers, therefore, were generally creating a more practical fashion, more realistic and less formal, while still maintaining elegance and refinement – women tended to become more women and less divas.

In 1966, a prestigious Italian manufacturer, Visconti di Modrone

Gianni Versace, costume sketches for Salomé.

Gianni Versace, evening gown.

Romeo Gigli,
embroidered brown velvet vest.

Romeo Gigli,
shawl made of embroidered violet velvet.

Romeo Gigli,
cape made of plaited velvet ribbons.

Ungaro, afternoon outfit.
Fall-winter collection 1992-1993.

Yves Saint Laurent, velvet outfit.
Fall-winter collection 1987-1988.
Photograph by Gian Paolo Barbieri.

Yves Saint Laurent, colored velvet outfit.

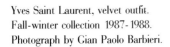

(among other things the first company to launch – in 1972 – pieces of a meter and a half in width, as opposed to the more conventional size of ninety centimeters) manufactured "Ducaflex" a "decoupé" cotton velvet, marked by its extreme elasiticity and wrinkle-proofing[25]. And so it happened that this fabric was used together with jersey and flannel, "moiré" and furs in a broad range of possibilities that seemed endless, as in the leather and velvet overcoat, made by Redaelli for Yves Saint-Laurent at the end of the Sixties[26].

Valentino added to velvet embroideries in silk, for example, in the cape of the fall-winter season of 1967, evoking the mosaics of the Domus of the Dioscuri, in Rome, or else in the evening jacket from the spring-summer season of 1968, made specifically for Audrey Hepburn and inspired by the elegance of traditional Spanish costumes[27].

Up until the mid-Seventies, the only real trend-setters were high fashion and boutique fashion, both areas of luxury goods, intended for a very limited buying public. Most women tended to rely on their local family dressmaker, who copied the patterns published in magazines. Mass production, which was still anonymous, tended to emphasize nothing so much as the limitation of costs, with no particular concern for quality or fashion. Later on, the spread of wealth and the growth of the consuming public led to the gradual development of prêt-à-porter, the industrial production of clothing which, unlike production, former series tended to bear the name of an already established designer.

The development of large-scale industrially manufactured fashion, capable of meeting the demand of the market sector that was not served by high fashion or boutique fashion, even changed the structure of the textile manufacturing companies, modifying both their manufacturing processes and their distribution and policy of corporate image. By virtue of the relationship that had been established with the prêt-à-porter apparel industry, through the role of the designer, the textiles manufacturers realized that they would have to begin performing a new type of research, with a view to diversifying their products on a seasonal basis, within strict limitations of scheduling and cost. The codified image of high fashion, which made obligatory choices in its selection of materials, was now offset by the extreme mobility of prêt-à-porter, which was distinguished by the continual process of exceeding its own limits, in the unending search for new technical and esthetic alternatives, capable of stimulating the market.

In the specific field of velvets, the process of industrialization had established the need to produce bolts that were 140 centimeters in width for women's clothing and 150 centimeters for men's clothing, in place of the more standard bolts measuring 75 centimeters for corduroy and 90 centimeters for smooth velvet. In the Seventies, this aided a large-scale revival of velvet. Natural fibers, in particular, were enjoying a comeback due to the economic crisis and sharp rise in the price of petroleum products, established by OPEC countries, which damaged the synthetic fibers industry.

As early as the previous decade, the Redaelli company, working far ahead of its times, had produced great quantities of cotton velvet, such as "Magia" and "Street Velvet", destined for use by the apparel industry. Now, however, chiefly due to innovations by the French, first among them Yves Saint-Laurent, the relationship between designers and textiles manufacturers became increasingly close. Velvet was featured, to great acclaim, in the new collections of prêt-à-porter, which thus took from high fashion the prerogative for use of this fabric, leading to industrial production of velvet in unprecedented quantities. The runway presentations of Saint-

Christian Lacroix, evening wear outfit.
Fall-winter collection 1989-1990.

Gianfranco Ferré, velvet outfit.
Fall-winter collection 1988-1989.
Photograph by Herb Ritts.

Givenchy, evening gown in black muslin,
with velvet trim.
Fall-winter collection 1992-1993.

Valentino, evening gown, haute couture.
Fall-winter collection 1992-1993.

Valentino, evening gowns, haute couture.
Fall-winter collection 1991-1992.

Velvet made of stamped viscose.
Redaelli Velluti Collection, 1990.

Laurent during these years featured cocktail outfits both for evening wear and for day wear, with a masculine cut, long overcoats with impeccable and geometric lines, outfits for day wear with patchwork effects, all of which served to update velvet, making it extremely wearable.

The folk style, moreover, along with the trend of revivals, both of which were driving styles in the fashion of this period, contributed to the spread of velvet in women's clothing in the more non-conformist versions. Russia and China both intrigued designers, with features that were borrowed and applied with unerring taste and humor. After the Far East, Spain's turn came, followed by Mexican gypsies, Indian clothing, and the traditional costumes of the Balkans. In particular, Lancetti offered a great variety of interpretations of these themes with his creations, taking advantage of the qualities of "au sabre" velvets or "imprimé" velvets, with their strong and exotic shades.

While in the women's fashion of the Seventies what prevailed was, as always, smooth velvet, as opposed to corduroy, in men's fashion there was a general conquest – in the jackets and especially in trousers – of the casual style and, with it, corduroy, which best corresponded to the new life styles. But with Gianni Versace's menswear collection of 1982, which took its inspiration from Calabrian popular culture, and featured velvet effects of multiple cords and Prince-of-Wales relief, a period of innovative solutions came to an end, and a new and more difficult period began, in which the market was clearly saturated, and so remained until 1987.

Manufacturers and designers believed that the fashion of corduroy had come to an end, and that this fabric, now old and thoroughly "passé", was no longer capable of generating new ideas and trends. It was chiefly the result of the excessive marketing of the Seventies, and of low quality, which had ruined the image of corduroy. Only smooth velvet, as opposed to corduroy, had managed to maintain a certain stability, particularly in the field of women's wear, both because of the greater range of diversification of products as compared with the sector of menswear, and because of its unrivalled status as the leading fabric in the most elegant articles of clothing. Valentino, for example, throughout the entire decade, made constant use of velvet in his evening wear, making good use of its most traditional qualities. Gianni Versace, on the other hand, in his incessant experimentation with materials, made use of a new stretch velvet, made by Redaelli, which was a perfect exemplification of the blend of wearability, high technology, and originality in his collections.

The fall-winter season of 1982-1983 represented a particularly significant moment in the use of this fabric, but it was chiefly from the end of 1988 on that a rediscovered taste for the past and for tradition began to be made manifest, accompanied by a growing desire for ornamentation and opulence. The shift toward a neo-baroque fashion and toward a more marked femininity, underscored by the adherent and close-fitting lines of miniskirts, tube skirts, and leggings, brought with it the large-scale revival of smooth velvet, especially in its elastic version. Velvet for a total look, which includes elegant suits and outfits and sports jackets, with the juxtaposition of fine cords with elephant cords and other larger cords, smooth surfaces and bark-like effects, all in an endless blend of colors.

In the men's fashion of 1989, the designers adopted, for the sportswear line, extremely loose and comfortable versions of velvet, obtained through special washing techniques, or they made use – Gianfranco Ferré was a perfect example – of smooth velvet (as opposed to corduroy) printed with Prince-of-Wales and pied-de-poule patterns. For evening wear and for formal occasions, though

Moschino, evening wear outfit.
Fall-winter collection 1993-1994.

they may be more casual, silk velvet – printed with small and fine paisley designs or tie patterns – was used almost without exception, tone on tone, for jackets, trousers, and vests[28].

Velvet offers a certain irony concerning the luxury of jackets adorned with braiding or other trim, and made more dramatic by the choice of darker colors. Purple, plum, coal grey, and curry were the shades that best exalted the effect of the shiny and the opaque, the iridescent effects of velvet, renewing a certain dandyfied tradition with patinaed, jacquard, and overdyed effects[29]. In women's fashion, in the Nineties, the manufacturers tested new and intriguing processes. The all-important factor is the quality of splendid shiny silk velour, like the "moiré" from Redaelli for Saint Laurent, adorned with the embroideries of Lesage. Another set of features are the virtuoso effects of gauffered velvet, which emulates the pleats of the Fortuny style in the evening outfits and capes from Romeo Gigli, with their opaque and dusty colors[30]. With a view to that trend, Legler designed for the 1990 season an exclusive "Stone-cord" – a special finish gives the velvet an effect of aging, while through unprecedented effects of chromatic contrast, softened tones were attained. An exclusive product of the Lanificio Loro Piana was an unprecedented cashmere velvet, made up of 80 percent cotton and 20 percent cashmere. Precious and refined, it was presented in the classic "cord" version, but development is underway on a broader range, covering all the different arrays of corduroys.

The efforts made over recent years by the weavers to revive the sector and to update processes and treatments seems to have yielded the results that were hoped for: velvet is experiencing one of its better seasons in fashion.

Pierre Balmain, evening wear outfit.
Fall-winter collection 1991-1992.

Montana, afternoon wear outfit.
Fall-winter collection 1989-1990.

Nina Ricci, evening wear outfit.
haute couture.
Fall-winter collection 1992-1993.

Givenchy, evening wear outfit,
haute couture,
top made of embroidered velvet.
Fall-winter collection.

Lacroix, velvet shawl.
Fall-winter collection, 1989-1990.

Notes

1. *L'eleganza delle stelle*, in *Lidel*, 15 March 1931, pgg. 46-47.

2. *Le velours. Tissu roi de cet hiver*, in *Vogue* (France), October 1932, pgg. 34-35.

3. *Hommage à Elsa Schiaparelli*, exhibition catalogue, Paris, 1984.

4. B. Giordani Aragno, *Le avanguardie della moda dal 1930 ad oggi*, in *Le fibre intelligenti. Un secolo di storia e cinquant'anni di moda*, edited by M. Garofoli, Milan, 1991, pgg. 105 f.

5. G. Butazzi, *1922-1943. Vent'anni di moda italiana*, exhibition catalogue, Florence, 1980, pgg 26-27.

6. E. Corvini, *Profili della moda avvenire*, in *Vita tessile*, February 1941, pgg. 75-80.

7. G. Nicodemi, *I velluti italiani decorativi*, in *Snia Viscosa. I nuovi tessili*, year III, October-December 1937 (XVI), no. 13, pgg. 18-25.

8. Vanessa, *Le straordinarie risorse del velluto inammaccabile*, in *Vita tessile*, March-April 1941, pgg. 128-129.

9. In *Vita tessile*, June 1938, pgg. 41-42 and December 1939, pgg. 34-35.

10. *Velvet, Fabric of Aristocracy since days of Antiquity Breaks the Traditional Spiral of Fashion Renaissance*, in *American Fabrics*, no. 10, 1949, pgg. 78-83.

11. J. Stephane, *L'hiver et les nouveaux tissus*, in *L'Officiel*, no. 413-414, September 1956, pgg. 232-241.

12. *Robe de soir 1850-1990*, exhibition catalogue, Paris, 1900.

13. *Hommage à Christian Dior 1947-1957*, exhibition catalogue, Paris, 1986, pgg. 43, 58, 146-151.

14. *Ibid*, pg. 181.

15. *Hommage à Balenciaga*, exhibition catalogue, Lyon, 1985, pgg. 49-57, 112-113.

16. In *L'Officiel*, no. 413-414, September 1956, pg. 332.

17. A. Fiorentini Capitani, *Le carte vincenti della moda italiana*, in *Sala Bianca. Nascita della moda italiana*, edited by G. Malossi, Milano, 1992, pgg. 112-114.

18. In *Novità*, no. 194, May 1963, pgg. 60-61.

19. A. Fiorentini Capitani-S. Ricci, *op. cit.*, 1992, pgg. 105-112.

20. In *Novità*, no. 72, October 1956, pg. III; *Novità*, no. 108, October 1959, pg. XXIII.

21. *Le lane e i velluti cambiano aspetto*, in *Il Mondo tessile*, year VIII, no. 6, 1953, pgg. 221-224.

22. *Regards sur les tissues d'hiver*, in *L'Officiel*, no. 473-474, September 1961, pgg. 106-113.

23. *Givenchy. 40 ans de création*, exhibition catalogue, Paris, 1991, pgg. 59-64.

24. Misia, *Alla sesta manifestazione fiorentina della nostra moda*, in *Il Mondo Tessile*, year VIII, no. 6, 1953, pgg. 248-250.

25. *Vogue e Novità*, year II, 1966, pg. 84.

26. *Vogue* (America), 15 September 1969, pg. 90.

27. *Valentino. Trent'anni di magia. Le opere*, exhibition catalogue, Rome, 1991, vol. II, pgg. 76 no. 47, 83 no. 62.

28. *Cosa ne dicono...*, in *L'Uomo Vogue News*, November 1989, pgg. 44-47.

29. *Velluto Anni '90*, in *L'Uomo Vogue News*, November 1989, pg. 48.

30. In *Collezione Donna*, no. 11, Fall-Winter 1989-90, pgg. 194-199.

Bibliography

L'eleganza delle stelle, in *Lidel*, 15 March 1931, pgg. 46-47.

Le velours. Tissu de cet hiver, in *Vogue*, October 1932, pgg. 34-35.

L. Putell, *Torniamo all'antico*, in *Per Voi Signora*, February 1932, no. 1, pgg. 2-3.

G. Nicodemi, *I velluti italiani decorati*, in *Snia Viscosa. I nuovi tessili*, year III, October-December 1937 (XVI), no. 13, pgg. 18-25.

Vita Tessile, June 1938, pgg. 41-42.

Vita Tessile, December 1939, pgg. 34-35.

E. Corvini, *Profili della moda avvenire*, in *Vita Tessile*, February 1941, pgg. 75-80.

Vanessa, *Le straordinarie risorse del velluto inammaccabile*, in *Vita Tessile*, March-April 1941, pgg. 128-129.

Velvet, *Fabric of Aristocracy since days of Antiquity Breaks the Traditional Spiral of Fashion Renaissance*, in *American Fabrics*, no. 10, 1949, pgg. 78-83.

Le lane e i velluti cambiano aspetto, in *Il Mondo tessile*, year III, no. 6, 1953, pgg. 221-224.

Misia, *Alla sesta manifestazione fiorentina della nostra moda*, in *Il Mondo tessile*, year VIII, no. 6, 1953, pgg. 248-250.

J. Stephane, *L'hiver et les nouveaux tissus*, in *L'Officiel*, no. 413-414, September

Novità, no. 72, October 1956, pg. III.

Novità, no. 108, October 1956, pg. XXIII.

Regards sur le tissus d'hiver, in *L'Officiel*, no. 473-474, September 1961, pgg. 106-113.

Novità, no. 194, May 1963, pgg. 60-61.

Vogue e Novità, year II, 1966, pg. 84.

Vogue, 15 September 1969, pg. 90.

Tema costume interpretato con spirito moderno, in *Linea italiana*, 1970, pg. 3.

G. Butazzi, *1922-1943. Vent'anni di moda italiana*, exhibition catalogue, Florence, 1980, pgg. 26-27.

Hommage à Elsa Schiaparelli, exhibition catalogue, Paris, 1984.

Sorelle Fontana, exhibition catalogue, Parma, 1984.

Hommage à Balenciaga, exhibition catalogue, Lyon, 1985.

Pierre Balmain. *40 Années de Création*, Paris, 1985.

Donazione Tigelli. La vita del costume, il costume della vita, Milan, 1986.

Hommage à Christian Dior (1947-1957), exhibition catalogue, Paris, 1986.

La Moda italiana, Milan, 1987, vol. II.

L'Uomo Vogue News, November 1989, pgg. 44-48.

Collezioni Donna, no. 11, Fall-Winter 1989-90, pgg. 194-199.

Robe de soir 1850-1990, exhibition catalogue, Paris, 1990.

S. Kennedy, *Pucci, A Renaissance in Fashion*, New York, 1991

A. Fiorentini Capitani, *Moda italiana. Anni Cinquanta e Sessanta*, Florence, 1991.

Théâtre de la Mode, exhibition catalogue, New York, 1991.

Givenchy. 40 ans de crèation, exhibition catalogue, Paris, 1991.

Valentino. Trent'anni di magia. Le Opere, exhibition catalogue, Rome, 1991, vol. I.

B. Giordani Aragno, *Le Avanguardie della moda dal 1930 ad oggi*, in *Le fibre intelligenti. Un secolo di storia e Cinquant'anni di moda*, a cura di M. Garofoli, Milan, 1991, pgg. 105-204.

A. Fiorentini Capitani-S. Ricci, *Le carte vincenti della moda italiana*, in *Sala Bianca. Nascita della moda italiana*, edited by G. Malossi, Milano, 1992, pgg. 87-122.

The periodicals

Tessili Nuovi, from 1948 to 1954.

Bellezza, from 1947 to 1963.

Krizia, matching trousers and jacket.
Fall-winter collection 1993-1994.

Max Mara, evening wear outfit.
Fall-winter collection 1991-1992.

THE COLOR OF RUBY RED

Luisella Pennati

La Scala, Milan, 1989-1990.
The stage, with the setting for *I Vespri Siciliani*.
Photographic Archives of Teatro alla Scala, Milan.

From its very first appearance in the theaters of the western world in the fourteenth century, the response was unanimous: velvet certainly knew how to do its job. After seducing kings and queens, it proffered itself to princesses and emperors and then went on to win the hearts of popes and great warriors, who competed in spectacular rivalries in elegance, striving to attain and then show off the most modern and exquisite versions. And ever since then, velvet has clothed the powerful and enveloped lovers, and it has been dyed in colors strong and subtle, in order to reflect the evanescent light of the real moon and to reflect the brighter glitter of the false moons of stages in theaters. And when the kings and queens stepped down from their thrones and emerged from their castles, treading the boards of theaters to entertain the masses, velvet was the uncontested champion of fabrics, winning a central and dominant role in the staging of a new form of theater, opera. It was there that velvet found its assigned playground, where actors could spin in its smooth folds, and where it could drape and enfold and drop majestically, adorning the royal box or the balconies in the hall; velvet girded itself with polyurethanes and dacrons so as to cover the seats in the orchestra with a ruby red coat of smoothness, the smaller seats in the balconies, and the highest perches of the "gods". Velvet appeared and disappeared as it was transformed into the curtains that long since replaced – in almost all of the theaters of the world – the painted backdrop. And velvet has even learned to meet with the strictest regulations on fireproofing and fire retardants, in order to maintain its access to its preferred place of pride in the theater.

It could be due to the fact that by intensifying or diminishing its weft, it is possible to regulate the acoustical absorption of sounds, or it may be because its luminous softness irradiates an intriguing sensation of pleasure – in any case, one thing is certain: velvet, in its most widespread version, in a ruby red color, with occasional descents to the hues of carmine red, and the rarer excursions to the original shades of blue-green, has adorned the halls of the most famous theaters in the world.

It is well known that in the international panorama of great opera houses, Italy is the true kingdom of theaters. After inventing "teatro all'italiana" in its classic architectural form, it was exported everywhere in the world, from the countries of eastern Europe to the United States and Latin America. Beginning in the eighteenth century, almost every theater in the world adopted velvet both as the prime fabric for the decorations and the furnishings of the hall and for the curtains.

The architectural structures of theaters before then (such as the sixteenth-century Teatro Olimpico in Vicenza, by Andrea Palladio, built with an open wooden *scenafronte*, the theater of Sabbioneta by Scamozzi, and the seventeenth-century Teatro Farnese in Parma, by Aleotti) although they are all unquestionably jewels of theatrical architecture, due to their extraordinary conception of space and the relationship between the hall and the stage, still take their inspiration from the Greek and Roman models of the amphitheater, and thus there are neither curtains nor seats. Beginning however with the eighteenth-century Teatro alla Scala, in Milan, built by Piermarini; the Teatro La Fenice in Venice, by Selva; the nineteenth-century Teatro Massimo Bellini in Catania, by C. Sada, to the very latest, the Teatro Carlo Felice in Genoa, by Aldo Rossi and Ignazio Gardella (which is not even to mention the theaters of Naples, Palermo, Caserta, Florence, Bologna, Parma, and all of the others), velvet confirms with its ubiquity how indispensable an element it is in theater design, due to design decisions of a technical, functional, and esthetic nature.

Teatro Carlo Felice, Genoa.
Design by Aldo Rossi, Ignazio Gardella, Angelo Sibilla, 1990.
The auditorium and the stage.

In the case of Genoa's Teatro Carlo Felice, for example, the opera house built to designs by Aldo Rossi and Ignazio Gardella and inaugurated in 1990, extensive acoustical studies of the hall confirmed that velvet made with pure mohair wool constitutes the perfect upholstery for the seats, even for an opera house of innovative design, as is the Carlo Felice, with its walls sheathed in bardiglio. The Redaelli Company, in the design of the velvet used to upholster the chairs, employed a smaller number of wefts than is normally used, with a view to ensuring in any case a satisfactory acoustical response in the hall, both in cases in which the hall is packed with people and in cases in which the hall is almost empty. Lighter-weight velvet was instead selected for the area behind the "palchetti", or auditorium boxes while for the curtain, constructed with the classic house draw-curtain opening, the choice fell on a flame-resistant velvet in pure mohair wool, of over 800 grams per square meter.

All over the rest of the world, the choice of velvet was confirmed once again, both in old theaters and in those built over the last decade, with only a very few exceptions. We find it in the Sao Carlos of Lisbon; the Gran Teatre del Liceu, in Barcelona; the Opera of Montecarlo; the Opera Garnier in Paris; the Royal Opera House at Covent Garden, in London; the Wiener Staatsoper; at the Opera de la Monnaie in Brussels; the Deutsche Staatsoper in Berlin; the Markgraefisches Opernhaus in Bayreuth; in almost all of the other theaters in Germany; the Magyar Allami Operahaz in Budapest; the Kungliga Teatern in Stockholm; and at the Bolshoi Theatre in Moscow; as well as at the opera houses of the New World, such as the Metropolitan of New York, the Teatro of Manaus or the Teatro Colon of Buenos Aires, and a great many others.

Shall we provide just a few examples?

The Opera de Versailles, the court theater built at the behest of Louis XV and designed by Jacques Ange Gabriel, was the largest theater in France prior to the Opera Garnier. Recently restored to the original cold chromatic shades that Louis Philippe had replaced with what was at the time a more up-to-date color scheme of red and gold, the theater is marked by decorations in faux marble and a capricious counterpoint of drapery and scrolls in turquoise-colored velvet, topping the closed curtain. In the hall, a few harlequin-colored references serve as ornamentation to the balustrades.

The Markgraeflisches Opernhaus in Bayreuth, the hall that Wagner favored before he began to plan his own opera house, seems to be an enlargement of an eighteenth-century diorama. The hall, designed and decorated by one of the scions of the famous dynasty of the Galli-Bibiena, Giuseppe, tends to favor cold colors, among them a hushed blue-green, with which the few surfaces left free of a curious baroque gilt are adorned. The complex teaser of the curtain develops its drapery over different levels: the exquisite quality of the fabric and the richness of its use on different levels makes this display of velvet particularly effective. The same velvet covers the backs of the chairs, which can be seen from the balustrade of the auditorium boxes.

Striking and soft is the use made of this fabric in the hall of the Opera of Montecarlo, designed by Charles Garnier, the architect of the Opera of Paris. Velvets and brocades are balanced in a counterpoint, a chromatic duet of reds and yellows, draping the Prince's Box in a frontal perspective, with the stage and the arches that open along the sides of the hall. The overall effect of splendor and priceless decorations attained is not detached from the technical effects, by which the velvets serve as screens for the arched openings of the hall, with a virtual reconstruction in acoustic terms.

Théâtre de l'Opera, Versailles.
Design by Jacques Ange Gabriel, 1770.

Markgraefliches Opernhaus, Bayreuth.
Design by Giuseppe Galli Bibiena, 1757.

Grand Théâtre, Bordeaux.
Design by Victor Louis, 1780.

Cuvilliéstheater, Munich.
Design by Franois Cuvilliés, 1753.

A triumph of red velvets for the seats, auditorium boxes, railings, and the remarkable French-style curtain in one of the most eclectic Grandes Salles in any theater in the world: Palais Garnier. Designed in the style of Napoleon III by Charles Garnier, the hall of the Opera has been enormously popular with the theater-going public of Paris ever since its opening.

Charging the velvet with the added value constituted by the choice of the color red, Garnier claimed that he had relieved the faces of the ladies in the audience of those unhealthy reflections that suggested an advanced state of ill health, the responsibility for which lay entirely with the shades of green that had been selected for the upholstery and curtains. The new complexions and the naked shoulders of the ladies in the audience, illuminated with new-found vitality, could thus better perform their duties as decoration, which function the ladies were called upon to serve in their auditorium boxes, where they were summoned to offer themselves to the public view.

Garnier's influence was felt as far away as the Kungliga Teatern in Stockholm, where velvet is present in a curtain that is allowed to buckle, offering draperies and festoons adorned with gold fringe. A well balanced counterpoint is provided by the seats in the hall and by the loggias that punctuate the balconies with the distinctive swan's-neck partitions in red velvet.

In the Cuvillietheater in Munich, the use of velvet is actually simulated. During the war, this theater enjoyed a remarkable form of protection: it was in fact entirely dismantled and was then reassembled, on a larger format, at a different location. In the sumptuous baroque hall, dripping with gold decorations, the draperies are sculpted and painted red, in emulation of the real velvet, each detail with a different plasticity, and left draped over the railing of the balustrades. These latter features constitute a further decorative instance, which is added to that of the red velvet of the seats in the hall and the boxes.

The Bolshoi Theatre ("bolshoi" means 'large'), which seats two thousand, is of a Neo-Classical style, and is of the same age of Milan's Teatro alla Scala. Rebuilt in 1856 in the wake of a terrible fire, and the home of the prestigious ballet company which has performed throughout the world, the Bolshoi has hosted – amongst the purplish red of the velvets and the glittering gold that adorns the hall – some of the most important historic meetings, such as that of the Soviet Congress, or that of 1922 in which the Soviet Union was proclaimed.

This tour of the world's theaters could continue, but in order to illustrate a small emblematic piece of the history of these prestigious theaters, facing as they do so many management problems, social and economic problems, all quite similar and all inevitably overcome in the name of music, we have decided to take as emblematic the history of one of the great artistic uses of velvet in one of the most celebrated theaters in the world: the Teatro alla Scala in Milan.

The Great Hall

The Hall of the Teatro alla Scala, in Milan, was not designed by Piermarini with the current decorations. Over the course of time, it had undergone a certain number of revisions, renovations, and restorations, up until the total rebuilding following the bombing in 1943, which was to transform the Hall into the current-day splendid vessel of spectacles and dispenser of dreams. Dreams of ruby-red velvet, evoked by the drapery on the boxes, the upholstery of the seats, the carpeting, the pleats and teasers of the curtains.

A brief historical review may help the reader to form a more complete idea of the Great Hall.

On 26 February 1776, the Ducal Theater of Milan burned down. After the serious but hardly uncommon accident (theaters in those days, built out of wood and with backdrops in cloth or paper, were lit by candles, and quite often went up in flames), the Milanese commissioned the architect Giuseppe Piermarini to design the building for a new theater. Taking an extremely rapid and courageous decision, the city of Milan decided, surprisingly, to build not one but two theaters: the Teatro Grande alla Scala and the Piccolo Teatro alla Canobiana, now the Teatro Lirico Internazionale, standing on another plot of land in the general vicinity of the former Canobian Schools. The design and the estimates were delivered by Piermarini in mid-September 1776, and on 3 August 1778, just twenty-nine months later, a performance of the "Europa Riconosciuta", by Antonio Salieri, inaugurated the new theater.

What immediately caught the general attention about the new building was its architecture, the size of the hall, and the ingenious devices with which the stage was equipped. The hall was originally built with four orders of boxes, with the bottom three orders already under option for those financing the new theater, the former box-holders at the Old Ducale. Then there was a fifth order and the top gallery, or the "gods". Once the purchase had been made, then each new owner hurried to decorate his or her new box and emblazon it with emblems according to the customs of the time, furnishing it with tables and chairs, transforming the box into a full-fledged private drawing room with cunning little curtains of taffeta, good for a number of purposes. Behind these curtains, visitors could be received, arguments held, the famous yellow Milanese risotto could be cooked; and sometimes, excessively amorous trysts were organized, acting out that which in Italy were the most important scenes in the setting: love.

As Stendhal describes it in an amusing letter to his sister Pauline, "in the two hundred tiny drawing rooms that overlook the hall and which are called 'palchi', or boxes, from their windows adorned with little curtains, conversations are carried on, and refreshments are brought to the ladies..." As early as 1830, however, the smoke from the candles and from the little stoves installed in the backs of the boxes forced the directors of the theater to carry out a major renovation of the great hall; on that occasions the excessively multi-colored decor of the hall was modified. The architect commissioned to do the job was the refined stage-designer Alessandro Sanquirico, who was responsible for the almost-total renovation of the great box of the Imperial Royal Court and of its upholstery and textile decorations. Sanquirico replaced the taffeta with decorations in crimson silk velvet and ermine, trimmed with fringes, cords, and gold tassels.

Concerning the color of the cloth making up the curtains of the existing boxes, the architect noted that, taken individually, he found them "handsome and well designed", but that if he had been asked

La Scala, Milan.
View of the interior of the theater, 1830.
Museo Teatrale alla Scala, Milan.

La Scala, Milan.
View of the facade and the side of the Teatro alla Scala, from Contrada Santa Margherita.
Museo Teatrale alla Scala, Milan.

to consider them as decorations for two hundred boxes, all in one place, he had to describe them as an "incomprehensible mishmash". The Duke of Visconti, the representative of the Imperiali Regi Teatri, or Imperial Royal Theaters, then established a rule that the curtains had to be made "with a single major piece of cloth, dropping in the middle, with a tail on either side, all in the same color, sky blue", upon assurances from Sanquirico that this would have an excellent overall effect, since he had seen it work in other theaters.

This was a period in which the Theater lived intensely, not only because it was in use almost every evening (the schedule included more than two hundred performances every year, not including the parties, in masquerade and not), but because it had become the center of all social life. Representatives of all of the classes of the city appeared at performances at La Scala, divided according to status by the architectural heirarchy of the hall, which assigned places according to caste – orchestra, first second and third orders of boxes, and the gods – but in any case all in the same place, forming a curious and variegated human landscape.

The boxes, owned by the aristocrats or upper-middle class, could be considered miniature theaters where the owners played the role of minor stars. The ladies knew everything there was to know about the behavior that was appropriate, and about its effects upon the designated victims. Transposing the inner and outer spaces, the stage was transferred inside the box, and the performances that went on there could be viewed from the hall (provided of course that one chose to make that performance visible), or else they could be hidden from outside view by closing the curtains, if one desired to conceal everything in total intimacy or else carry out more complex amorous strategies.

In an effort to find some remedy for these customs, the authorities issued a decree according to which "during the performances, the boxes must all be open, save for cases of mourning, of which however the directors of the theater must be notified in a timely manner". Specifying that the "opening of the curtains must take place half an hour before the performance begins and can be closed only after the performance ends", the authorities were doing their best to reduce the risk that there would be more and more "boxes of the widows".

At the end of the spring season of 1844, the director of the Imperial Royal Theaters, decreed: "The Government, having determined to put into a more pleasant and decent condition, for the coming autumn season, the curtains of the boxes of the Regio Teatro alla Scala (Royal Theater of the Scala), which have by now been reduced, by use and by the passage of time, to a state of filth that is no longer compatible with a Royal Theater, (one wonders what must have become of the "sky blue" prescribed by Sanquirico?), has decided to have them recolored in a bright capercaillie wood-grouse color (sic!), since this is the color that proved most effective and positive in the various tests that were made, and which is, at the same time, most suited to the general system of decorations. The directors of the Imperial Royal Theaters... therefore requests that the Owner of the Boxes in the theater in question be so kind as to follow the example that the Government has already set in the boxes of its own property, themselves immediately arranging for the coloring of the fabrics that make up the current curtains and coverings of their boxes; we advise them, simultaneously, for their own information that the Government has made use of the work of the fabrics manufacturer Signor Lamberti, who lives in the Contrada del Cappello no. 4026, and who will, for the cost of between ten and twelve Austrian lire per box, including installation, be happy to accept the greatest variety of commissions. On the premises of the same is a sampling of the decorations in the new colors on display, and it is not allowed for the box-owners to stray from said range of samples, due to the necessary uniformity of all decorations. The Imperial Royal Counsellor of Government and Director, Crippa". And with this stroke of the pen, the hall was decorated with upholstery in a handsome green color, like that of the wood grouse.

In 1897, La Scala was forced to close down, due to a lack of funds. The poster bordered in the black of mourning, placed by an anonymous Milanese, said: "Closed due to the death of the sentiment of art, of city pride, and of common sense". The theater then underwent a number of different misadventures. But the most serious damages resulted from the Second World War, with the bombing of 13 August 1943. Between 1943 and 1946, the engineer Luigi Lorenzo Secchi oversaw the total reconstruction of the hall, including the upholstery in red damask of the walls and of the ceiling of the boxes and the valances, in ruby red velvet. These remained until 1988, the year in which there was a general renovation of all the fabric furnishings of the hall, including the curtains of the royal box and of the other boxes.

La Scala, Milan.
The Royal Box, 1988.
Photographic Archive of the
Teatro alla Scala, Milan.

The seats and the carpeting

It was a custom for the public in the orchestra section to watch the performance standing up. In the context of the overall innovations of 1830, it was decided to equip the orchestra section with numbered seats, emphasizing the central passage and leaving some standing room at the rear of the hall. This standing room was definitively abolished in 1891, the year in which other seats were added to increase the number of seats and satisfy the demands of growing audiences.

Beginning with the earliest years of operation, dating from its foundation in 1893, the Redaelli company established itself as one of the most esteemed suppliers of the Teatro alla Scala. In 1910 the old wooden seats were replaced with a new model of seat, which respected the regulations in terms of size. In the years that followed, the administration of La Scala worked hard on the renovation of the stage, with such projects as the lowering of the orchestra pit, moving the forestage back, the installation of equipment for lifting heavy objects, fire-fighting, and heating and electrical systems. Then, in August of 1943, La Scala was destroyed, and was subsequently rebuilt, with completion in 1946.

During that period, maintenance was extremely careful but none too frequent – in fact, it was not until 1969 that the administrative council of the Agency in charge of La Scala, which had been an independent body for some time, voted to replace the seats and the carpeting. The job fell to the engineer Secchi, in his role as Conservator, to arrange to draw up the commissions to be assigned to specialized companies, who were invited to bid both for the task of supplying new padded seats, entirely upholstered in ruby red velvet, and for the carpeting, which was to be manufactured with felt made of pure virgin wool, with a base completely free of synthetic threads. so as to prevent the accumulation of static electricity that might damage the acoustical effects. The wool was dyed specially so that it would harmonize with the ruby red velvet of the seats.

The rest is recent history – during the height of the wave of corporate sponsorships, Enichem offered, in August of 1988, an opportunity to the superintendent, Carlo Maria Badini, to arrange for the total replacement of the fabric hangings and upholstery of the hall.

Contracts were drawn up for the partial replacement of the paddings and velvet of the seats – the weaving mill of Nole supplied approximately 1,800 meters of mohair velvet with pure virgin wool fleece of the finest quality, free of tanning wool, dead wool, regenerated wool, animal bristles, chemical or vegetable fibers, and with a base structure of fire-resistant fibers. In compliance with the current laws and regulations, the carpeting was supplied, made with specially dyed polyamide fibers, by the Lanerossi company of Vicenza. The Great Hall was beginning to take on the appearance that is now so familiar to us.

The great velvet curtain and its forerunners in painted cloth

A movable partition between the portion of space that constitutes reality and that other portion of space in which illusion is interpreted, the curtain made its debut in the chronicled accounts of the Festa del Paradiso which Leonardo da Vinci prepared in the Castello Sforzesco in 1490 for the wedding celebrations of Giangaleazzo Sforza and Isabel of Aragon. The curtain was opened and closed manually, and this opening did not occur through the curtain being pulled open from the center toward both sides, nor through its being raised, but rather through the brusque and sudden collapse as it was

La Scala, Milan.
The velvet curtain and the auditorium boxes, 1988.
Photographic Archive of the Teatro alla Scala, Milan.

La Scala, Milan.
Il Parnaso, the first curtain painted by Donnino Riccardi,
on a theme suggested by Giuseppe Parini, 1778.
Museo Teatrale alla Scala, Milan.

View of the Teatro alla Scala with the curtain by Angelo Monticelli, 1821.
Museo Teatrale alla Scala, Milan.

unhooked from the rafters, as we would say today. It dropped into a "director's pit", and this usually happened with a tremendous boom. The ensuing shock, followed by a pause, during which there were no actors on stage, prepared the audience for the coming performance. Then the curtain was no longer used until the end of the performance.

From the construction of the Teatro Farnese onward, the curtain took the following form: a great painted cloth, framed by the proscenium, in which there were two doors, one through which the actors could enter the stage and another through which they could return to the stage to take their bows. The curtain remained in view until the end of the symphony or the prelude, thus establishing a powerful presence in the hall, and then as it rose it punctuated the beginning and the end of the fable.

For the first big curtain of 1778, a competition was run based on a play by Parini, and was won by Donnino Riccardi. Normally, in fact, it would be a specially formed commission that would see to the selection of the subject. For the second curtain, the work of Angelo Monticelli, with the title of "The Arts and the Sciences Work to Perfect Italian Theater", dated 1821, there is a rough sketch by the author and prints from the time, which show the curtain set in the stage. It was used until 1862, the year in which it was ordered replaced because of its state of disrepair, since it could no longer be kept lowered at the beginning of performances, and could only be lowered at the end of the performance "as if it were an evil witch, designed to chase off the spectator". The last painted curtain, "Le Feste Atellane", was the creation of Giuseppe Bertini, and was executed on the basis of a sketch taken from the work of Raffaele Casnedi.

With the year 1889, the end of the century drew near, and the painted curtain gave way to an innovative curtain made of ruby red velvet bordered with gilt fringes, devoid of all decoration so as to become an integral part of the furnishings of the hall – it works to counterbalance the red of the auditorium boxes, lined with equally red damasks and crowned by velvet drapery; this "closed" the hall. The qualitative aspects of the velvet ensured that it would survive until 1976, almost a hundred years!

When the time came to replace the velvet, the engineer Lorenzo Secchi recalls that "there were considerable difficulties encountered and overcome in succeeding in finding the linen velvet that had the same qualities of weave as in the curtain that had lasted for nearly a century. Italian and foreign weavers were contacted, and all of them... declared that it was practically impossible, nowadays, to weave velvets with the same procedures that were allowed by hand-operated looms. Finally, patient and insistent research led La Scala to a Venetian weaver, Rubelli, which out of love for La Scala agreed to weave the velvet ... and dye it ... so that the new curtain could attain the same presence in the great hall as if it had always been there".

It had just been hung, on 7 March 1976, when a sudden outbreak of fire on stage on the afternoon of 4 February 1977, managed to destroy it together with the musking, another subsidiary curtain in golden yellow velvet, and various other stage material. That evening, the fifth performance of "Norma" was cancelled – all of La Scala's staff worked continuously until the following evening, achieving a sort of miracle, and on the evening of 5 February the "Moses and Aaron", went on as scheduled. In 1988, the year of the theater's renovation, the Way company, an accredited manufacturer of curtains for La Scala, received delivery of the ruby red flame-proof velvet material used to make the current curtain. It was made like a domestic draw curtain with decorations of braiding and gold "lamé" foil and cotton thread and cascades of fringe.

*Congiurati
Tedeschi*

Caramb
'913

Barma
Bonomini
Nicolini
Martegani

Galliera
Cassinari

The stage costumes

Velvet was used in the decorations of theater halls, but it was also used to an overwhelming degree on stage in the costumes of the artists. Here velvet had a variety of incarnations – it was gathered, engraved, curved, cut intricately, printed, adorned, and painted. By capturing the glare of the spotlights and dominating that light, velvet was used to sculpt jackets, corsets, doublets, dress-coats, petticoats, mantels of all sorts, doing all that it could to transform costumes, at times turning them into full-fledged masterpieces. What importance does a stage costume have? An enormous importance. And we can learn this from Giuseppe Verdi, by reading the interesting and extensive correspondence that he carried on with Giulio Ricordi, writing three thousand five hundred letters in fifty-five years!

Milan, 1886, in the days preceding the premiere of "Otello".
- St Ag(ata) 18 Oct 1886
Dear Giulio,
... reconsider the last sketch for Othello. It is beautiful, but it is not credible! It is a Teodoros Negus... a Cetivayo (save for the paunch), but it is no Othello in the service of Venice.
G. Verdi
(editor's note: the costume sketcher was Edel)

Milan, 23 October 86
Illustrious Maestro
... I called for Edel, and I will see him today or tomorrow: I will explain to him what you want for the latest costume of Othello...

Sincerely yours,
Giulio Ricordi
Wednesday, 4 o'clock

(Busseto/3 Nov/86)
Dear Giulio,
...I have seen the sketches and I still find the latest one of Othello to be too savage*... nothing Venetian about him at all... Desdemona too is excessively lavish in the first Act. The others are fine and the sketch for Iago is excellent.
* moreover, it attracts too much attention and is a distraction. If the Audience reaches the point of saying "Oh what a handsome costume" we are done for. Artists must have the courage to "s'effacer"!! Tomorrow I will write you once again.
G. Verdi

It may seem strange, at first, for us to realize that with all the problems of music, orchestra, and musicians, primadonnas and singers that were plaguing Verdi, he still found the time to write so many letters to change the cut of a costume. But it is not that strange after all – the Grand Old Maestro knew perfectly well that opera is theater of extremely delicate architecture in its composition – one mistaken variable and that unique brew loses all its magical properties.

The costumes created for the theater live from the moment in which the show begins and in part die with the end of the performance, disappearing into the labyrinths of storage, in storage closets that stand thirty feet tall or stacked in boxes, if these are old performances, and seeking them out is like looking for a needle in a haystack.

It may therefore happen that one stumbles upon the costume that Maria Callas wore in the role of Rosina, with a sense of good luck, joy, and excitement, or it may happen that nothing comes down off the shelves at all, because the show – in the words of Nicola Benois, creator of costumes for 250 performances – "was recycled in the name of economy – almost always misguided and not always justifiable – so that an entire group of costumes might be destroyed in order to obtain the material 'needed' for a new performance.

Which is not even to mention the fact that surprises can treacherously emerge from the closets as well – just when one thinks that one has found the costume so long sought after, the realization dawns that it is not the original costume at all, but the product of subsequent modifications applied in various instances, in order to be worn by various singers and actors. Some of the most wonderful velvet costumes, sought with great determination and effort, and finally found, now have a name and an owner. Each costume, with its own history, has served to adorn remarkable and successful artists, as well as great artists who have not enjoyed success. Or else second-flight singers, less well known, that for a thousand reasons of life, have played the roles of stars or extras. Their photographs, arranged chronologically, stealing a little bit of the show they appeared in, let us relive an instant of the Fedora, a snippet of Macbeth, or a moment of Rigoletto.

Not without allowing us to admire an array of sketches, illustrating creative phase that goes prior to the creation of the costume designed by such remarkable artists as Caramba, who imprisoned in velvet the different characters of so many different operas. Caramba's designs have a remarkable freshness and vitality that distingish the character while hinting at his or her role, and they are often endowed – not only with the various annotations – but also with samples of the velvet chosen for the final version.

Let the curtain go up on this small gift to the Theatrical Costume!

On pages 158- 160- 161:
Luigi Sapelli, known as Caramba.
Sketches, 1913.
Museo Teatrale alla Scala, Milan.

Nobili
Spagnuoli

Caramba
1913

Caramba
913

Caramba
913

Caramba
1913

Caramba
1914

The Costume of Giuditta Pasta
as *Anne Boleyn*
for "Anna Bolena", by G. Donizetti

Teatro Carcano, Milan, 26 December 1830
Teatro alla Scala, Milan, 25 February 1832

In the scene in the last act of "Anna Bolena",
just before the heroine mounts the scaffold, with
the celebrated aria, "Al dolce guidami castel na-
tio...", Giuditta Pasta is portrayed in an ample
and lavish sixteenth-century outfit made of silk
velvet; the outfit is stark and black, and "in it she
will die". The abundant sleeves with satin lining
and with slits from the shoulders down under-
score the desperation indicated in the gestures of
the arms. The image is the same as that success-
fully captured in the splendid oil painting by Carlo
Bruellow, long hanging in the villa at Blevio owned by the singer, and now in the collection of the
Museo Teatrale alla Scala, in Milan. It was with
the first performance of "Anna Bolena", written
by Donizetti between 10 November and 10
December of 1830 that Giuditta Pasta made her
triumphant debut in Italy. She was already well
known outside of Italy, but not in Milan, and the
remarkable singer was engaged by the Teatro
Carcano to open the opera season in December of
1830. She was in competition with another celebrated singer, Giuditta Grisi, who that same
evening was singing in "Capuleti e Montecchi", by
Bellini, in the opening performance of La Scala.

Despite expectations to the contrary, which
called for the triumph of La Scala and of Bellini's
opera, the most enthusiastic responses were for
the Carcano, with the debut of Donizetti's new
opera and the new singer. La Scala put on the
opera in 1832, but did not enjoy the same degree
of success as the Carcano.

Giuditta Pasta in *Anne Boleyn* by Gaetano Donizetti.
Teatro alla Scala, Milan, 25 February 1832.
Carlo Bruellow, oil on canvas.
Museo Teatrale alla Scala, Milan.

The Costume of Maria Malibran
as Desdemona,
for "Otello", by G. Rossini

Teatro alla Scala, Milan, 20 May 1834

On the evening of 20 May 1834, Maria Felicia Malibran sang in Rossini's "Otello" at La Scala, in the role of Desdemona. She was spectacularly successful, and the celebrations continued even after the end of the performance in the garden of the home of the Duke Visconti, a great admirer of the soprano. The party held on that unforgettable evening in her honor culminated in a serenade written by Romani, the text of which was distributed as a souvenir to all of those in attendance. "The voice of voices", as the poet Carlo Angiolini described her after a performance, then decided to pose for the painter Luigi Pedrazzi, wearing her marvelous stage costume of crimson-colored silk velvet which had brought her so much luck. What emerged was an oil painting that portrayed an extremely gentle Malibran with a hint of melancholy mischief, an anti-diva in her goddess-like costume of red velvet. What is the meaning of the flowers that she holds in her hand in the painting? The flowers are a camelia, an acanthus, a rose, a hops flower, and an olea fragrans – in Italian, they form an acrostic giving the name of Carlo, the name of her great love, the violinist Charles de Beriot.

Maria Felicia Malibran in *Othello* by Gioacchino Rossini.
Teatro alla Scala, Milan, 20 May 1834.
Luigi Pedrazzi, oil on canvas.
Museo Teatrale alla Scala, Milan.

**The Costume of Maria Meneghini Callas
as *Anne Boleyn*
The Costume of Giulietta Simionato
as Jane Seymour
for "Anna Bolena", by G. Donizetti**

Teatro alla Scala, Milan, 14 April 1957

In the 1956-1957 season, with the staging of
"Anna Bolena", in the edition that bore the name
of Gavazzeni, Visconti, and Benois, starring Callas
and Siminato, the opera, after eighty years of
oblivion, entered the history of opera as a legendary performance.

Nicola Benois, under the direction of Visconti,
and perhaps taking inspiration from the painter
Hans Holbein, designed extremely refined and
sumptuous costumes with a soft, sixteenth-century cut. He chose to make the costumes out of
purple silk velvets bordered with colored crystals,
for the spectacular Jane Seymour, played by Giulietta Simionato, "marvelous to see and splendid
to hear", an authentic lover of Henry VIII.

For the first and second act, for the star, Anne
Boleyn, instead, two splendid dark-blue velvet
costumes were created, with ample sleeves lined
with satin, adorned with crystals and tear-drop
pearls.

But it was for the last act that Benois reserved
his masterpiece of a costume, or at least the outfit
that Maria Callas loved best – the death robe. The
simple vest was remarkably adorned by a long
black train – and from that velvet emerge notes of
true poetry, nostalgia, and pathos, that the great
artist succeeded in transmitting to the audience,
even when taking bows or embracing Simionato
after the performance, or, they say, even now,
when her ghost wanders across the stage, where
so many claim to have seen her.

The Costume of Lucia Valentini as Angelina for "Cenerentola", by G. Rossini

Teatro alla Scala, Milan, 19 April 1973

On the night of 19 April 1973, Lucia Valentini Terrani, just twenty-seven at the time, and barely three years into her career, attained her dream of singing at La Scala in the starring role of "Cenerentola", by Rossini. The lavish costume of black and gold velvet that Angelina/Cenerentola received as a gift, not from the fairy godmother, but rather from the tutor of the prince, so that she could take part in the ball, was based on a sketch by Jean Pierre Ponnelle, who oversaw the direction, the stage design, and the costumes of this performance of "Cenerentola".

Of curious eighteenth-century cut, with the outlandish plumes that seem to be a reference to vaudeville or burlesque, the costume "abundantly covered the ankles" and was spectacular in the effect it made on stage.

Ah the ankles! The librettist, in order to reconcile the papal censors, did not think it right for the female lead to show her ankle in trying on the other slipper of the famous fairy tale, and therefore replaced the token of love that she was to leave the prince – no longer her slipper, but rather her bracelet.

Lucia Valentini Terrani in *Cenerentola* by Gioacchino Rossini. Teatro alla Scala, Milan, 19 April 1973. Photographic Archive of the Teatro alla Scala, Milan.

The Costume of Ciro Ruffo
as the Stand-In for the King
for "Il Viaggio a Reims", by G. Rossini

Teatro alla Scala, Milan, 9 September 1985

Il Viaggio a Reims, or L'Albergo del Giglio d'Oro was the last Italian opera that Rossini set to music, with great inspiration and a certain degree of opportunism, in order to reinforce his already well established reputation in the French court, where festivities were underway for the coronation of Charles X. The presentation at La Scala left an indelible impression in the minds of the Milanese. It is time for the aperitivo in Milan – everyone is outdoors enjoying the sunset after a beautiful day. From Piazza Scala set out the procession of the king to be crowned, Charles X, alias the mime Ciro Ruffo, who made his way with some difficulty amongst the crowd in an effort to travel the stretch of road from Piazza Scala to the church of San Fedele. Here he was crowned, and then he had to make his way back to the Galleria and then into La Scala theatre.

A great many recall the red streak of a crimson velvet mantel, extensively adorned with gold, which the king, with a none-too-regal cigarette in his mouth and an eccentric entourage of ladies and knights in costumes made of taffeta and unforgettable velvets, showed while trying to keep up with the ushers of La Scala making way amidst the crowd so as to reach the church for the coronation. In the end, he succeeded, and reached the theater where a cheerful brigade of international opera stars had waited for him till then, waiting impatiently to leave the Albergo del Giglio d'Oro to make their way to Reims.

The mime Ciro Ruffo in *Viaggio a Reims* by Gioacchino Rossini.
Teatro alla Scala, Milan, 9 September 1985.
Photographic Archive of the
Teatro alla Scala, Milan.

The Costume of Montserrat Caballé
as *Mary Stuart*
for "Maria Stuarda", by G. Donizetti

Teatro alla Scala, Milan, 13 April 1971

The costume worn by Mary Stuart in the presentation at La Scala in April of 1971, not unlike that worn by Elizabeth I, was designed and assembled with a cunning and effective use of velvets and lace.

If the stage design had a vague sense of deja' vu, it was no doubt the product of the many years of collaboration between the stage designer, Nicola Benois, and the director, Margherita Wallmann, and certainly not because of the costumes, entirely original and specially designed for this staging of the opera.

Conceived in a different manner, from the point of view of the colors as well, intended to highlight the contrasts between the personalities of the two queens who played leading roles, the costumes by Nicola Benois are rich in gold trim and edging, intended to highlight the late sixteenth-century line constituted by brocades and embroidered velvets which appear from the waist down.

The Catalonian soprano Montserrat Caballé, dressed in velvet, appeared on the stage as "fiercely bellicose as ever, in the spirited leaps of a voice that tugs, plunges, and rises majestically in an admirable idealization of grief, as well as ferocity". (Corriere della Sera, 14 April 1971, F. Abbiati)

The Costume of Juan Pons
as Sir John Falstaff
for "Falstaff", by G. Verdi

Teatro alla Scala, Milan, 7 December 1980

"That Mister Ford is an ox! and as an ox I shall fit him with horns. You shall see! But it is late. Wait for me here, and I shall go and prepare myself".

And, thus singing to Mister Ford who has approached Falstaff under false guise, Sir John Falstaff exits in order to "sharpen his weapons", in preparation for his romantic encounter with Alice Ford.

He returns just a little later with a new waistcoat and breeches of a deep pink color, a hat with an array of manicolored plumes, a walking cane, and an ample mantel made of velvet of a wine-colored chenille.

"I appear quite the rooster in this costume!" said Juan Pons-Falstaff to his true wife. "And so it must be!" she responded, clearly referring to the implicit ambiguousness.

Falstaff is the star, and the only character that the set designer Ezio Frigerio puts into a costume of such comical pretentiousness in the setting of healthy country manners, transported from the Windsor of the fifteenth century to the foggy Po Valley.

With the Juan Pons of this staging of the opera by Verdi, conducted by Maazel with Strehler as the director, and a lively and brilliant Mirella Freni as the female lead, the opera has finally rediscovered its Falstaff, the ideal leading man that it had lost after Mariano Stabile left the stage leaving no heirs, after last performing under the baton of Arturo Toscanini on 26 December 1921, for the inauguration of the Ente Autonomo Teatro alla Scala, first public opera house in Italy.

Juan Pons in *Falstaff* by Giuseppe Verdi.
Teatro alla Scala, Milan, 7 December 1980.
Photographic Archive of the
Teatro alla Scala, Milan.

**The Costume of Shirley Verrett
as Lady Macbeth
for "Macbeth", by G. Verdi**

Teatro alla Scala, Milan, 7 December 1975

During the preparation for the staging of Macbeth, Giuseppe Verdi spent months of time and produced mountains of director's notes, among other things, expressing his determination that the producer use silks or velvets for the costumes.

One hundred twenty-eight years later, Damiani, who was entrusted with the creation of the stage settings and the costumes for Macbeth in 1975, directed by Strehler and conducted by Abbado, ignored his orders, or perhaps obeyed him more than anyone else had.

For the two starring roles, in fact, he chose extremely long mantles, "signs of nobility, power emphasized to the point of excess, and long trains that during the on-stage action became as twisted as snakes..." – and he did all this with the very material that Verdi had rejected, velvet.

But he treated it as if it had become an anti-velvet: chenille, crushed and hollowed out, dragging, dyed a hot coppery rust color, with an extremely contained decorative mark that made the two starring figures clearly stand out as anti-kings.

Verdi wrote: "And I want Lady Macbeth to be evil and unsightly... a Lady that does not sing... in this Lady I want a harsh, strangled, dark voice... I want there to be something diabolical in the voice of this lady".

And she was found! Verrett as the star of this opera was a Lady Macbeth that was "stupefying in her musical beauty, intensity, and stage presence".

And if she was the Lady Macbeth, Macbeth himself was played by an unforgettable Piero Cappuccilli, in a remarkable performance.

Shirley Verrett and Piero Cappuccilli
in *Macbeth* by Giuseppe Verdi.
Teatro alla Scala, Milan, 7 December 1975.
Photographic Archive of the
Teatro alla Scala, Milan.

Bibliography

A.A.V.V., *Enciclopedia Garzanti della musica III Edizione*, Albo Garzanti Editore, Milan, 1974.

A.A.V.V., *La Danza, il Canto, l'Abito: costumi del Teatro alla Scala 1947-1982*, Silvana Editoriale, Milan, 1982.

A.A.V.V., *Lo Spazio, il Luogo, l'Ambito. Scenografie del Teatro alla Scala 1947-1983*, Silvana Editoriale, Milan, 1983.

A.A.V.V., *La forma dinamica dell'opera lirica: regie del Teatro alla Scala 1947-1984*, Silvana Editoriale, Milan, 1984.

G. Strehler, E. Frigerio, *L'atelier dell'illusione: Teatro alla Scala, quarant'anni di costumi*, Valentino Garavani, Milan, 1985.

G. Tintori, *Lettere dal Teatro: collezione del Museo Teatrale alla Scala*, Imago, Milan, 1983.

G. Tintori, *Cronologia: opere, balletti, concerti 1778-1977. Duecento anni di Teatro alla Scala*. Grafica Gutenberg Editrice, Gorle (BG), 1979.

L. L. Secchi, *1778-1978, Il Teatro alla Scala*, Electa Editrice, Milan, 1977.

G. Verdi, G, Ricordi, *Corrispondenza e Immagini 1881-1890*, Edizioni del Teatro alla Scala directed by Carlo Mezzadri, Milan, 1981.

A.A.V.V., Programmes of the Teatro alla Scala concerning the performances: *Anne Boleyn*: Teatro alla Scala, Milan, 13 April 1971; *Cenerentola*: Teatro alla Scala, Milan, 19 April 1973; *Macbeth*: Teatro alla Scala, Milan, 7 December 1975; *Falstaff*: Teatro alla Scala, Milan, 7 December 1980, *Il viaggio a Reims*: Teatro alla Scala, Milan, 9 September 1985; *Guglielmo Tell*: Teatro alla Scala, Milan, 7 December 1988.

A.A.V.V., *Opéras d'Europe*, Editions Plume, Paris, 1989.

TECHNIQUES AND TYPES OF VELVET

TECHNIQUES AND TYPES OF VELVET
Brief descriptive notes concerning the manufacturing processes mentioned and the technical terms used in the texts.
Roberta Orsi Landini and Alfredo Redaelli

I. THE CHIEF TEXTILE FIBERS

Textile fibers are generally divided into two major groups, natural and chemical. Natural fibers can be either vegetable, animal, or mineral. The chemical fibers, in turn, can be broken down into two groups: artificial fibers – of vegetable, animal, or mineral origins – and synthetic fibers.

1. Natural fibers

All of the principal natural fibers have been used in the manufacture of velvets throughout their history. Among those of vegetable origin, we should mention cotton and linen in particular. Cotton is obtained from filaments that coat the seeds of a plant from the mallow family (Genus Gossypium); linen comes from the stalks of the Linum usatissimum plant. Velvets made of plant fibers can definitely be documented as far back as the eighteenth century, often in the form of plushes (Appendix VI, 11). The production of cotton velvets acquired increasing importance from the nineteenth century onward, with the invention and diffusion of mechanized looms; this fabric was at first used chiefly in interior decoration, but from the turn of the century onward it made its way into the apparel market as well.

Linen velvet, which was used most widely in interior decorating, enjoyed its greatest success in the 1960s.

Among the various animal fibers, wool – obtained as we all know from the fleece of members of the sheep, goat, and camel families – was certainly used in velvets as early as the eighteenth century (Utrecht velvets), in the field of interior decorating. From the second half of the eighteenth century onward, it was also produced in a number of prestigious textile-manufacturing centers, such as Paris, Tournai, and, in Italy, Florence, on velvet looms for specific types of moquette carpets. Nowadays, high-quality mohair yarns are used in the manufacture of velvets suited for the upholstery of the interiors of trains and theater seats.

The history of velvet is, at any rate, the history of silk velvet. Silk threads are obtained from the cocoon of a worm, the Bombix mori, which emits extremely fine filaments which are gathered in the operation of silk reeling and are then twisted to make the very fine thread stronger. The silk is then washed and degummed in order to make it soft and shiny. For velvet pile, the legislation of the Guilds required the very finest silk thread, organzine, which is obtained by twisting together two or three yarns in the opposite direction from the orientation of each of them; thus a very thin, yet strong and elastic, thread, perfect for warps was obtained. Currently, schappe is widely used for the pile of expensive velvets; schappe is obtained from the first raw waste of silk production.

Natural mineral fibers, above all gold and silver, enter the production process of velvets generally in the form of gold and silver threads, wire or filé, as supplementary decorative wefts, which play no role in the real structure of the cloth.

2. Artificial chemical fibers

These are obtained from the spinning and coagulation of substances of vegetable (cellulose) or animal (protein) origin.

The various types of rayon (a continuous fib-

The silk reeling:
manual processing of the cocoon.

er yarn) – viscose, cuprammonium rayon, and acetate – are derivates of cellulose, which is made spinnable through specific chemical processes. Viscose rayon, the most common, dates from 1885; cuprammonium rayon was perfected by J.P. Bemberg (from whom it takes its name of bemberg in Italian), in 1892; while acetate rayon (the most common italian commercial names are Rhodia and Albene) dates from 1894. The success of the various forms of rayon and their use in the manufacture of velvets, similar in appearance to silk, dates from the Twenties. Artificial chemical fibers of vegetable origins have made it possible to produce velvets of excellent quality at reasonable prices, allowing a diffusion and use, in apparel and interior decorating, that is extending to ever greater areas of the market. In its special version frayed fiber with permanent curling – greater ability to withstand wear and strain, often with an opaque appearance – viscose rayon has proven to be an excellent thread for the manufacture of velvets for interior decoration.

Artificial fibers of protein derivation (Lanital, derived by Snia Viscosa in 1935) are generally not used in the production of velvets, but are chiefly used for knit products.

3. Synthetic chemical fibers

Depending on the synthesizing process employed, chemical fibers can be classed as polyamides, acrylics, polyesters, polychlorovinyls, and polypropylenes.

The first to be synthesized were the polyamide fibers, which became successful beginning in the Forties. The first fiber, nylon, dates from 1931, and has been available commercially since 1939. Because of the properties of polyamides – enormous strength, resiliency, and tenacity – they were soon being used in the manufacture of velvets for interior decoration. The best known are Nylon, Delfion, Lilion. They have been used on occasion in velvets for apparel, but they have not enjoyed much success in that context.

Acrylic fibers too began to be used in the manufacture of fabrics for interior decoration, competitors of wool in terms of their lightness and resiliency, with names such as Velicren, Orlon, and Dralon. The best known polyester fibers, valued for their great strength and elasticity, are Terital and Wistel; in the production of figured velvets, at times polyester lamé thread, known as Lurex, has been used. Resistance to moisture is instead the salient characteristic of polypropylene fibers, derived from hydrocarbons (Meraklon). A few polychlorovinyl fibers, such as Clevyl and Movil, are used in flame-resistant velvets.

The threads of Lycra are used in the manufacture of elasticized or stretch velvets; Lycra was developed by DuPont – and was soon imitated by other manufacturers of fibers – with synthetic rubber.

II. THE MANUFACTURE OF A FABRIC

Fabrics are made up of two fundamental components: the warp and the weft, which intersect at right angles. Since there are a vast number of different ways in which the two component parts can be interwoven, there is a vast array of fabrics that can be thus created: plain fabrics are those whose surface presents a single weaving effect; figured fabrics are those in which decorated patterns and modular motifs are added to the basic weave. The latter fabrics are manufactured with looms that are equipped with more complex mechanisms.

1. Warps

The term warp refers to all of the threads running lengthwise that make up a fabric, each arrayed parallel to the others. The weaver or the weaving mechanism raises and lowers them, alternating them by group, with special equipment which can be varied, in accordance with the type of loom being used, so as to introduce the wefts between the threads of the warp, thus creating the weave. The threads of the warp, each perfectly separated from the others, and each of the same length and tension, are wound from one warp beam (with the shape of a roller) set in the rear of the loom all the way to another beam which is set before the weaver. Onto this beam the woven fabric is gradually rolled. Between the two beams, every thread of the warp passes through the meshes of one or more shedding devices which raise and lower it.

The preparation of the thread which must become a warp is called warping. By means of specific operations, groups of threads are wound onto the beam. The length, tension, and distancing are all perfectly regulated according to the type of fabric that is to be woven.

In complex fabrics, the ground or main warp is accompanied by one or more supplementary warps, which have different functions, and therefore different names. If a supplementary warp is used to create decorative effects, then it is called a pattern warp; if it serves the function of attaching, to the weave of the fabric, wefts that outline designs, then it is called a binding warp.

2. Wefts

The term weft describes the set or, or even just one, of the transverse elements of the fabric that are inserted, at a right angle, between the raised threads of the warp and those remaining stationary. In traditional looms, the weft is transported by a shuttle which contains the spool upon which the thread is wound. In modern looms, the shuttle has been eliminated: the weft is taken up directly by a distaff and is transported from one selvage to the other by means of pincers. A single weft is all that is needed in order to manufacture a simple fabric; in order to create motifs, one or two wefts are added to the main or ground weft: a supplementary weft that works from one selvage of the fabric to the other is called a pattern weft; when its movement is limited to the width of the area where it is required by the pattern the weft is called a brocading weft.

3. Weave

Even on the simplest of looms, the possibilities of weaving are extremely numerous, but

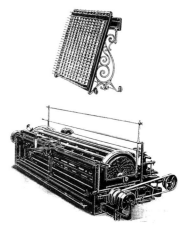

Sectional and fractional warpers, at Redaelli Velluti in different periods.

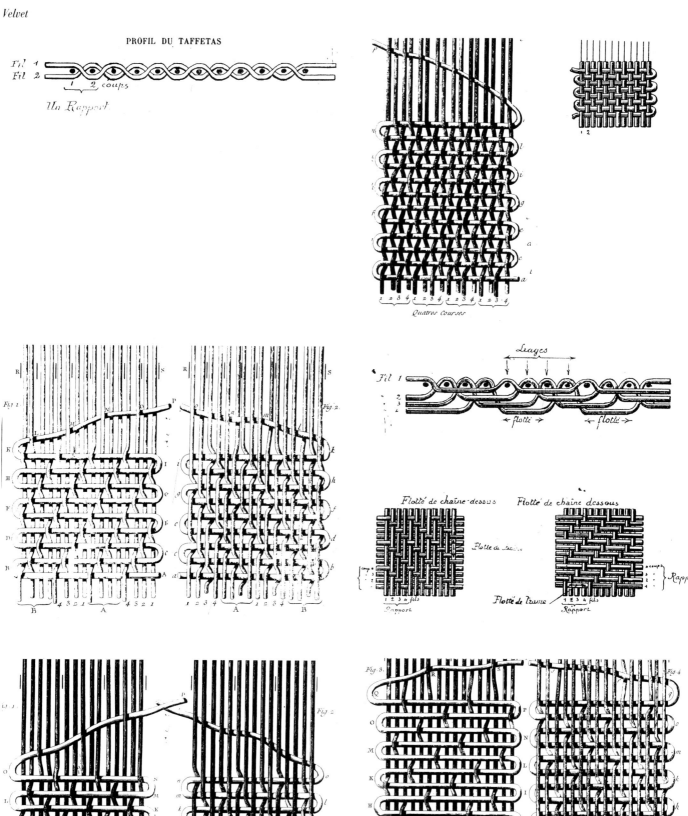

PROFIL DU TAFFETAS

Un Rapport

Quatres Courses

Liages

Flotté de chaine dessous   *Flotté de chaine dessous*

they all come down to one of three basic types: tabby or taffeta, twill, and satin.

4. Tabby weave

This is the simplest of weaves, with the wefts passing above and below each thread of the warp, alternating position with each subsequent passage. The front and the back of the fabric has the same appearance.
Taffeta is the term traditionally used for a silk fabric of tabby weave.

5. Twill

A system of weaving whereby the binding points (when the thread of the warp passes over the weft) are arrayed diagonally. If the appearance of the weft prevails on the front of the cloth, then the appearance of the warp will prevail on the back, and vice versa.

6. Satin

This is a weave, used by preference for silk, in which the warp tends to prevail on the front. The binding points are never adjacent, so as to create the appearance of a compact surface.

7. Loom

Machinery upon which the weave between the weft and the warp is constructed. It is equipped with devices that allow the threads of the warp to be raised in groups according to prior programming, so as to create different sheds into which the weaver inserts the weft by means of the shuttle. This equipment, in traditional looms, includes the shafts and heddles, which have an upper and a lower bar with a center loop called the eye, through which the individual ends of the warp are passed. The shafts are connected to threadles. Besides the shafts, the threads pass through the teeth of a reed, set on a comb beater, which keeps them at a regular and constant distance one from the other.

8. Draw loom

The mechanism known as the draw loom, which has not been used since the last century, made it possible to manufacture figured fabrics. In the draw loom, groups of threads of one or more warps were inserted in the heddles, as well as in the figuring harness.
These were raised, according to a program based on the design which was to be woven, by the drawboy, a laborer who worked alongside the weaver. The larger the module of the design, the more complex was the program, and the greater the value of the finished fabric. For velvets, each thread of the

On page 182:
Fundamental weaves: from top to bottom, tabby, twill, satin.

Drawloom.

Jacquard loom: detail. Arte della Seta Lisio Foundation, Florence.

pile warp passed individually through the eye of the leashes.

9. Jacquard loom

In a Jacquard loom, the first of which was put into operation in France in 1804, the programming of the design took place through the use of perforated pieces of cardboard which triggered the raising of the leashes; the draw boy, that is, a second worker who worked on the weaving of figured fabrics, was no longer needed. Production in this way became more rapid and less expensive, even though the insertion of the weft, that is, the true process of weaving, continued to be carried out manually for a great many years thereafter, at least for the most expensive fabrics.
Even today, for the creation of figured fabrics, the Jacquard mechanism, in far more sophisticated versions, is applied to modern looms.

10. Mechanical loom

In a mechanical loom, invented in the nineteenth century, all of the manual operations were replaced by movements of the machinery, driven by an engine. There was no longer any such thing as a true weaver. The weaver was replaced by the operator, who oversaw the correct operation of the loom. Mechanical looms can operate with or without a shuttle to transport the weft, the latter being a more recent development.

III. THE WEAVING OF VELVET

Velvet is a fabric whose surface is in part or entirely covered with pile. This effect can be obtained in any of a number of ways, either by means of supplementary warps or wefts.

1. Warp velvet

In the traditional manufacturing of velvet, on a drawloom, Jacquard, or double velvet loom, the pile is always constructed by adding a second warp to the main warp, which is in fact known as the pile warp; ancient or modern looms for the production of velvets were more complex than other looms, and the weaving techniques were very particular.

2. Pile warp

In hand-woven velvets, the pile warp is generally in silk, but it can be made with other threads, either natural or artificial or synthetic. The threads of the pile warp are either wound upon separate bobbins or else on special devices that keep each thread separate from all the others; they alternate with those in the main warp, in variable proportion according to the weave of the fabric. The threads of the pile warp are generally double or triple, so that they form, after the cut, a fuzzy surface that better covers the ground weave. In the standard width of the hand woven fabric (approx. 54-60 cm.), the overall number of threads in the pile warp generally ranges from 800 to 1,000 (13-16 per centimeter).

3. Rods

In hand-woven velvets, the pile warp is raised from the ground of the fabric by means of rods, during the weaving process. If these rods have a round cross section, then after they are inserted like a weft, they are subsequently withdrawn and they leave on the surface a loop effect (uncut velvet). In order to obtain, instead, a tuft effect, the rods that are inserted have a small channel at the top, within which the weaver inserts a small blade that cuts the threads surrounding the rod in two (cut velvet). Different forms, heights, and thicknesses of the rods can produce different effects of cut and uncut piles.
The rods used for the weaving of velvets are also used in some mechanized looms for figured double velvets.

4. Hand-operated loom for plain velvet

The hand-operated loom for plain velvet differs from a normal loom in that it has a supplementary beam set beneath the warp beam of the main warp, and in that there is a considerable difference in the tensions of the two warps – the main warp requiring a very great tension, and a very weak tension being required for the other warp, which must rise easily to surround the rods. There is further variation in the front beam, which causes the cloth to advance, and which may contain a special chamber so as to cause the velvet to proceed without crushing it, or which may be coated with a toothed metal surface which catches the fabric and holds it at the correct tension, while allowing it to fall freely in soft folds in a special box set beneath the cloth beam.

5. Double velvet looms

Beginning during the last century, a number of different systems have been devised for the manufacture of velvet – and a number of looms have been constructed – with a view to creating more rapid systems that would thus involve lower costs than the traditional methods. The necessarily time-consuming operation of inserting rods and making manual cuts for each rod has been eliminated by weaving two pieces of cloth simultaneously, keeping them one at the right distance from the other. The two cloths are held together by a single pile warp that passes from one weave to the other; a blade, mounted on a track, manages to cut the threads of the pile warp right in the middle, dividing the two fabrics and leaving upon each a velvety surface.

The idea of weaving two velvets simultaneously was developed in the earliest years of the nineteenth century; it was not until the 1830s that the looms had been perfected and patents had been issued for the processes that would ensure proper manufacturing results (see the history of the development of the velvet loom).

6. Loom for figured (Jacquard) velvet

For figured velvet, the loom is equipped with a special device, the creel, a sort of rack, which contains as many bobbins as there are ends in the pile warp. Each of them is therefore independent of the others, because it works separately according to the pattern in question. In hand-operated looms, each end of the pile not only passes through the heddles, but also passes through a mail of the figure harness linked to the Jacquard mechanism, which raises it as needed to create the design.

From 1837 onward, the Jacquard mechanism was applied as well on looms for velvets woven in double pieces.

7. Weft pile velvet

The idea of assembling a velvet by using the weft in order to obtain the tufts of pile and not a specific warp dates from the end of the eighteenth century.

IV. DYEING OPERATIONS FOR YARN AND PIECE FABRICS

The operation of dyeing serves to give the desired color to a textile fiber, of whatever sort.

The procedure involves the immersion of the yarn or fabric into a bath in which a colorant has been dissolved, and after a variable range of time, chemical products are added to the dye bath, so as to fix the color in the fibers; subsequently, abundant washing in water removes the excess color that has not been fixed.

In the past, dyestuffs were essentially derived from plants or animal sources; with the advent of petrochemicals, dyestuffs are now exclusively derived from petroleum byproducts. They are divided into different categories, each used for the dyeing of different fibers (natural, artificial, and synthetic).

The most important categories of dyes are as follows:

– Direct reactive dyestuffs based on naphta or sulphur, used for dyeing a number of different natural or artificial cellulose-based fibers.

– Acids and premetallized substances for

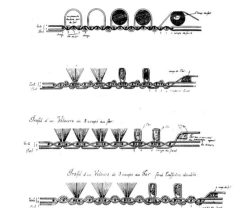

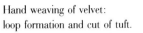

Hand weaving of velvet: loop formation and cut of tuft.

Hand-operated Jacquard loom for figured velvet. Arte della Seta Lisio Foundation, Florence.

wool and silk. Dispersed and basic dyes for synthetic fibers.

V. THE PRINTING OF FABRICS

Printing is effectuated by applying a colored paste to the fabric; and this can be done by means of pressure printing or through screen printing.

The printing paste consists essentially of coloring agents, used also in dyeing, specially thickened.

After the color is applied and fixed, the fabric is washed thoroughly in order to remove excess color and other substances, such as thickeners.

In direct printing, a coloring agent is applied to the colorless or dyed base fabric. In discharge printing (Rongeant), a special chemical substance is added to the printing paste; it is capable of destroying the color used for the basic dyeing of the fabric.

A mixed fabric made up of fibers of various sorts (animal, plant, or synthetic) can be printed with a product capable of destroying a certain fiber content of the fabric, thus creating a "devoured" or "devoré" effect.

Modern technology has developed printing procedures involving the transfer of a printed design from a substrate, usually paper, onto what are usually synthetic fabrics, by hot pressing the colored paper onto the fabric. This form of printing is usually referred to as transfer printing.

VI. VELVET MANUFACTURING: DYEING AND FINISHING

1. Yarn-dyed velvets

The rules set down by the Guilds of Silk-makers of the various manufacturing towns demanded in all cases for silk products of high quality, that the velvet should be yarn-dyed. Before the yarn could be steeped in the vat of dye, it was specially selected, all impurities were removed, it was degreased and washed with a series of operations that were very carefully regulated in order to ensure the highest quality and stability of the colors. Yarn-dyeing in is still used when the manufacturers wish to produce figured velvets with different colors for the gronud and for the pile, or else for velvets with two or three piles warps. Yarn-dyed velvets, therefore, require very few finishing operations, which in industrial production are pile shearing, pile brushing the opening of pile tufts.

2. Piece dyeing

Ever since the turn of the century, it has been common practice to piece dye viscose, cotton, and silk velvets, once it became equally common practice to use raw yarn in the weaving. For cotton velvets, generally

Detail of the creel. Arte della Seta Lisio Foundation, Florence.

Detail of the harness and the comb beater. Arte della Seta Lisio Foundation, Florence.

weft pile velvets, piece dyeing was already a process employed regularly.

The piece dyeing of velvet required special machinery that prevented the crushing of the pile. For heavier velvets or for pieces of greater length, the pad-steam dyer, or machine for continual dyeing, was used; for lighter velvets, the frame machine was used, which wound the piece in a spiral direction on a special structure called the star, due to its shape, and then dipped the fabric into a boiling dye in which the dyestuffs and fixing solutions were dissolved.

3. Brushing and shearing

The same machine can brush the pile in order to remove impurities from it and levels the height of the pile by means of one or two shearing cylinders, set in a line, and equipped with helical blades. The operation can be performed during the preparatory phase prior to the dye operation and during the finishing phase, following the shearing performed in order to remov the impurities or the dust derived from the brushing.

4. Wetting process

This series of operations is normally performed in sequence by a single machine called the Foulard, which conveys the piece through a bath in which wetting agents are dissolved in suspension, and then it runs the same piece between two cylinders that squeeze excess liquid from it, so as to make the moisture content uniform. This operation may also be performed prior to the dyeing operation, or it may become necessary during the finishing phase.

5. Finishing the velvet and opening of the pile tufts

Operations usually performed with a tenter machine equipped with brushing cylinders or with a series of carding and brushing machines set in a line; with this operation the pieces that have been washed and dried are stretched and brushed with steel brushes. The velvet, in this phase of manufacturing, can be impregnated with special chemical substances. During the drying process, the pile is brushed so that the tufts remain standing or in the positions required. In order to make the velvets more stain- and crush-resistant, or better suited for particular uses, the pieces of cloth are once again run through the finishing machinery, in order to impregnate them with solutions of synthetic resins which penetrate the fibers. The passage through the finishing and drying machine straightens the pile definitively, before the piece can be run through the high-temperature curer, where the resins themselves can be polymerized. The purpose of these treatments is to make the velvet – according to the specific features required – more resilient, water-resistant, stain-proof, or flameproof.

6. Special treatments and processing

Velvet, before or after the finishing process, can be subjected to further treatments and processing, such as: printing, embossing, by which process patterns are impressed by heat on the surface of the pile (gauffré); crushing and rumpling (froissé) by means of special machinery; pattern shearing, which cuts a pattern into the surface of the pile; the devoré processing of the pile, by means of a printing process that destroys the pile according to a design, forming a pattern.

VII. TYPES OF VELVETS

1. Cut velvet

This velvet has a surface covered with tufts of pile, which may cover it entirely in the case of solid or plain velvets, or else may be arranged so as to form a pattern, leaving part of the ground weave uncovered (cut voided velvet).

2. Pile-on-pile velvets with two or three heights

With the use of rods of varying thickness, patterns can be created with different heights of pile; the pattern on the fabric becomes three-dimensional, like that of a bas-relief. Likewise, with modern systems of cutting, velvets can be sheared with two- or three-pile heights.

3. Two-, three-, or four-pile velvets (polychrome velvets)

If two, three, or as many as four pile warps of various colours are used, the velvet becomes multi-colored and can produce magnificent and artistic effects. The number of threads in the pile warps doubles or triples in proportion, just as the number of spools on the creel does, and as does the number of mails; as a result there is a parallel increase in the time involved in the programming of the loom and the time required for weaving.

4. Uncut velvet

This is obtained through the use of rods with a round cross-section, inserted so as to raise the pile warp, and subsequently removed as the weaving operation progresses. This type of velvet can be solid or figured, even at different pile heights.

5. Ciselé velvet

This type of velvet has patterns in uncut and

An impregnation pod.

Star and dye vat in operation at Redaelli Velluti.

Pile embossing.

187

Redaelli Velluti, sample books, Fifties and Sixties.

cut pile, which, presenting different shades due to the differing refraction of light, create a variety of light effects. To these should be added the consideration of the different heights of the uncut pile with respect to the cut pile, which latter pile, due to factors in the weaving, always proves to be deeper than the uncut pile.

6. Brocaded velvet

The richness of the velvet is increased by adding to the base motifs created through the use of wefts brocaded in silver and gold. The technique of velvet brocades, necessarily executed on the front of the fabric, rather than on the reverse, as is common practice, proves to be particularly slow to be particularly time-consuming and complex, with a resulting increase in the value of the fabric, caused by the amount of intensive skilled labor as well as by the valuable raw materials.

7. Velvet "allucciolato"

This is the fifteenth-century term that describes the lighting effect produced by brocaded wefts amongst the velvet pile, when these wefts were, at regular intervals, raised with a rod in order to create scattered little loops of gold (bouclé effect). The same technique, when used with less valuable yarns, is still in use in certain areas where fabrics are still produced with traditional methods (for example, Sardinia and Apulia).

8. Velvet "a riccio d'oro"

In the velvets of the fifteenth and sixteenth century, in certain areas, brocades with gold and silver wefts, the wefts were raised as by the effect of "allucciolato", but the loops of gold are arranged densely one alongside the other in order to exalt the elements of the pattern. Thus, the three-dimensional effect obtained through the pile of the velvet, at times to various depths, is accompanied by the effect of the gold and silver loops, often manufactured in various depths and with a variety of threads.

9. Stamped or gauffered velvet

Used in the creation of decorative patterns on the pile of the velvet in an economic manner. The pile of a solid-colored velvet is crushed with hot metal matrices, leaving the pattern desired on the velvet. This is a type of velvet that has been manufactured since the sixteenth century; it is quite popular even today.

10. Chiné velvet

The technique for making chiné velvet involves dyeing of the warp, split up into little bunches, before placing it on the loom, with different and successive dye baths, so as to create a pattern. When the fabric is complete, the pattern is generally not perfectly defined in terms of borders. In order to dye the pile warp of a velvet with this technique – particularly slow and complex – it is necessary to accurately calculate the pattern extended lengthwise, in order for it to retain the correct proportions following the weaving. From the eighteenth century onward, the genuine technique of chiné, which involved a system of "reserve" dyeing, was replaced by the technique of printing on the warp, of relatively greater simplicity.

11. Plush

This is a variant of velvet, and it involves larger rods; therefore it has a deeper pile which is often less dense, and which can therefore lie along the surface of the fabric. It can be either solid or figured. It has certainly been in use since the seventeenth century. Beginning with the turn of the last century, plush was manufactured as an imitation of fur, and it has become fashionable again only recently, and is manufactured with special mechanized looms.

12. Miniature velvet

This name has less to do with the size of the pattern, and more to do with the technical refinement used in its manufacture. It often presents a multiple effect, such as two or three pile warps of different colours and laminated surfaces. Typical of the second half of the seventeenth century, when it was used in the most valuable men's suits.

13. Sans-pareil velvet

This is a velvet that features an uncut and a cut pile that both maintain the same height. There is consequently a variation in the method of weaving with respect to ciselé velvet, where the cutting rod rises above that of the loop and produces longer tufts. This is a velvet that emphasizes the lighting effects of the pattern, more than the relief effects. It was presented for the first time at the Paris Exposition of 1844.

14. Gandin velvet

This presents a pattern, not only on the pile, but also on the ground weave of the velvet. There is therefore a double set of harnesses for the ends of the ground warp and for the ends of pile warp. The system was invented at the turn of the nineteenth century; velvets with programming of the ground ends for brocading areas have been in existence since the XV century.

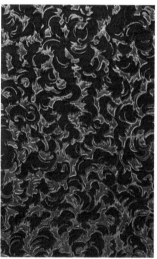

Redaelli Velluti, velvet made of acetate blend, for clothing, 1992.

Redaelli Velluti, embossed viscose velvet.

15. Bombé velvet

In bombé velvet, rods of different sizes are used to obtain the effect of transverse rounded cords. If the rods have special wavy forms, then instead of cords one would see rounded checks or rectangles. It has been in use since 1844 in a number of variants.

16. Chaméléon velvet

This is a velvet with an iridescent effect: the pile appears to be of two different colors, depending on the angle from which one looks at it. Of course, the manufacture makes use of two different pile warps in different colors and a special system of weaving. This was in fashion for men's and women's clothing from 1842 until 1846.

17. Au sabre velvet

Au sabre velvet is distinguished by the pile effects on specific areas of the fabric, often printed ones. It is not a true velvet; it is in fact a satin with a special weave; the pile, obtained when the cloth is finished, by cutting – by hand with a very sharp blade – the floats of the satin in the areas of the fabric where the design requires it. In use from the last quarter of the nineteenth century until the Second World War for prestigious items; also used in the production of ribbons.

18. Chiffon velvet

The weaving of velvet on a crêpe de chine ground dates from the turn of the nineteenth century, but it was not widely used, until a system was invented at the end of that century for using raw yarn in the weaving, leading to the creation of a great many new types of crêpe fabrics. Crêpes and velvets on a crêpes ground could be solid or figured, and in some cases printed with patterns. Incredibly light and soft, these were woven from the Twenties on with artificial fibers as well.

19. Devoré velvet

It is a velvet with an effect of differing weight of pile. It develops from the idea of partially destroying a yarn that makes up the fabric, leaving that yarn only in certain areas. It therefore becomes necessary to make use of artificial or synthetic fibers, along with a natural material such as cotton or silk; the artificial fibers during finishing are chemically dissolved along a pattern applied to the piece, by means of printing plates.

20. Velvet, velveteen

A cotton velvet obtained by cutting the weft floats after weaving. In velveteen, the weave

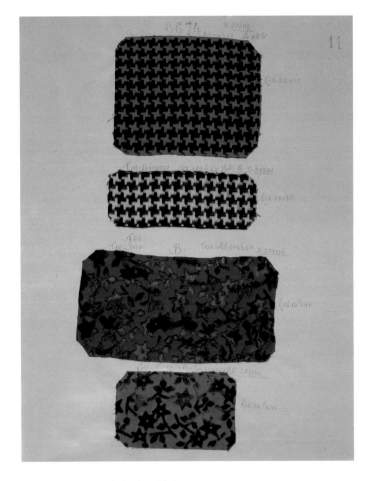

Redaelli Velluti, sample books, Thirties.

Redaelli Velluti, colour studies for Bayadera velvet.

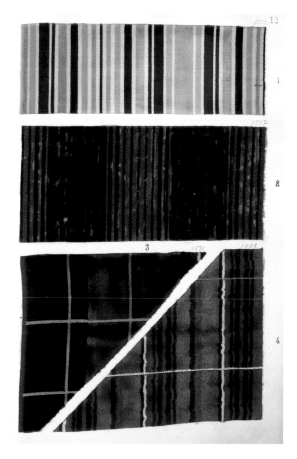

192   Sample book of Jacquard velvets. 1898-1899. Redaelli Velluti Collection.

Figured velvets made of silk, for clothing, Fifties. Redaelli Velluti Collection.

of the fabric is not unlike that found in reps, but the weft floats are arranged in declining order so as to better cover the weave of the fabric, after the cutting.

21. Corduroy

A cotton velvet in which the weft floats are arranged vertically, one above the other, so as to be cut lengthwise (inserting the weft floats under a blade in the nineteenth-century system; nowadays with a multiple mechanical cutting device). If the weft floats have different lengths and are arranged successively so as to increase or decline in number, then larger cords are created. The invention of corduroy seems to date from 1782, but it became particularly successful in men's sportswear in the nineteenth century.

22. Panné velvet

Velvet normally made with a viscose or silk pile, not at all bristly, and distinguished by its soft smooth appearance. It is made from a velvet with an upright pile; the velvet passes under a roller to flatten the pile.

23. Utrecht velvet

This velvet, used in home furnishing and in apparel, is at times voided or solid, with a surface entirely covered with a mohair pile.

24. Pékin velvet

Used in home furnishing and in apparel, this velvet is distinguished by vertical lines of pile of varied width separated by strips of plain weave, usually satin.

VII. TYPES OF FIGURED FABRICS MENTIONED IN THE TEXT

1. Samite

This is a figured fabric with weft effect. On the surface it features a diagonal weave and patterns highlighted by the interchange of two or more warps. A drawloom is required for the manufacture of this fabric. It has two warps: a main warp that is never seen on the surface of the fabric, but which serves to separate the wefts and cause them to appear or be hidden, according to the requirements of the design; and a binding warp that bound the wefts in twill. The most highly valued fabric of the Middle Ages, of which superb examples survive, of Persian, Byzantine, Muslim, and Lucchese workmanship. It has not been manufactured since the fifteenth century, when it was replaced by lampas.

2. Lampas

This is a figured fabric that has just two warps and at least two wefts. The ground warp works with one main weft, while the pattern is established by floats of pattern or brocading wefts, bound by the ends of binding warp (in a binding system), usually tabby or twill.

3. Brocatelle

This is a lampas with a ground weave in satin manufactured with a silk main warp and a main weft, generally in linen. The pattern is obtained with a silk pattern weft, bound in twill by a binding warp. The varying tensions of the warps create a distinctive relief effect, in which the areas in satin are raised and are seen as a pattern. This is a typical fabric used in home furnishing; it came in fashion in the sixteenth century.

4. Damask

This is a figured fabric that has just one warp and one weft, with motifs created by the opposition of two different weaves, generally the front and back of the satin. This fabric is used in furnishings, but with specific patterns; also used widely in apparel.

Corduroy for clothing.
Bonomi, Pontoglio, Visconti, TBM Collection.

Cord corduroys. TBM and Tronconi Collection.

Printed viscose velvets. Redaelli Velluti, 1989 Collection.

THE EVOLUTION OF THE VELVET LOOM
Alfredo Redaelli

Ever since its creation in the Far East, in China, a few centuries before Christ, and then later in Persia and in Asia Minor, with the Roman conquest, velvet was woven on simple hand-looms, where the rod, inserted every two or three picks, produced a little loop of pile; the cut would then take place through the insertion, into the small groove of the rod, of a hand-held knife, which the operator would then carefully run from one selvage to the other, cutting the loop and producing a pile surface. The production process was extremely slow and complex, but it remained unvaried for many centuries. At the beginning of the nineteenth century, a certain M. Dessuares, a professor of weaving theory in Lyon, developed the first system for weaving two superimposed pieces at the same time; this procedure made use of a simple loom, upon which, however, two pieces were placed one atop the other. The new approach consisted in the fact that the rod was inserted so as to pick up the pile for both fabrics at the same time, which meant that there was a considerable savings in time, as the operator could weave and cut the tuft of the upper and lower piece together. A catalogue of the exposition at Saint Etienne in 1891 mentioned a certain Monsieur Thiolliere David, who in 1793 had already devised the production of velvet woven in two superimposed pieces. It is interesting to note the way in which the new system for producing velvet in double piece immediately aroused the interest of European weavers at the time; a document dated 11 August 1808, from three Frenchmen named Charlier, Daber, and Remy, requested that the Minister of the Interior of Prussia-Rhineland issue a patent for the manufacture of velvet in double piece; this patent was indeed issued on 23 September 1808.

In 1853, the procedure, which had enjoyed some success and some failure, was adopted by Bezon, who perfected it. The manufacture of the hand-woven loom in double piece in effect reduced the production time for velvet by about 30 percent. Nevertheless, this procedure never managed to replace the traditional weaving process, inasmuch as the depth of the pile of the velvet of the lower piece was much greater than that of the pile on the upper piece, and no way could be found to solve this discrepancy. And so this process was abandoned.

Efforts to reduce labor resulted in researchers developing a new system of weaving, employing a completely new sort of loom that was based on the concept of weaving two fabrics, face to face, one atop the other, linked by a third warp, which was called the pile warp, and which was alternately interwoven in the upper and lower piece.

In 1824, a patent was issued to a gentleman named Steven Nelson for the "production of

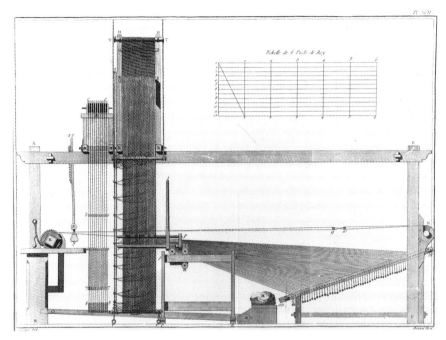

Hand-operated looms for figured velvet.

two pieces of velvet, joined at the face, and cut mechanically". A Frenchman named M. Ducis perfected this new idea around the year 1838, but the loom was still less than perfect, in that fabrics made with this new procedure still had to be separated, by cutting the pile ends that joined the two pieces after the weaving, when the fabric had already emerged from the loom, with another mechanism, also invented by Ducis. With this extremely important technological innovation, and thanks to the loom for double piece face-to-face velvet, we can say that the weaving of velvet entered the modern industrial age. A loom that no longer makes use of the "rod" for the formation of the velvet pile has a production of more than twice the traditional loom. Later on, two gentlemen of Lyon named Janin and Falsan began to weave velvet in double piece face to face by applying a device to the loom that had a knife capable of cutting the pile threads while still on the loom. The cutting operation, however, had to be performed after the weaving operation was halted.

Immediately following the development of this application, a gentleman named J.B. Martin, of Tarare, introduced an invention for which he received two patents. He had developed some important improvements on this loom; the most remarkable and productive improvement involved the process of cutting the velvet directly on the loom without interrupting the weaving process. This is the real first complete loom for double piece velvet, woven face to face. The quality of production obtained through this entirely new system was not, however, sufficiently reliable to ensure high-quality fabrics. The Spanish industrialist, Jacinto Barrau y Carter, of Barcelona, was said by some sources to be apparently the first manufacturer to produce a full-fledged mechanical loom for the weaving of velvet in double piece. In four years of intense work, he developed a mechanical loom that was patented on 28 October 1857 in Spain, and was introduced immediately afterward in France, Germany, and England. The quality of the velvet, especially in the area of the loom's cutting of velvet in double piece face to face represented an important step forward, with respect to the results that had been obtained in Lyon, and was based on the strength and durability of the component parts of the mechanical loom and the precision of execution. In those times the new mechanical loom in double piece was considered capable of hourly velvet production twelve times what could be produced with a traditional hand-operated loom. Barrau, however, had neglected his weaving business in order to work on his invention and, as a result, he was forced to sell the patents to his machine in order to survive. And in 1868 for Mr. Samuel Cunliffe Lister purchased the patents a mechanical velvet loom; he integrated and developed his velvet production, creating a huge company where, at the time, four thousand workers labored.

The mechanical loom invented by J. B. Martin and J. Barrau for the weaving of velvet in double piece face to face was distinguished by the fact that the wefts were inserted into both the upper and the lower pieces by a single shuttle, and the loom was equipped with a knife that separated the pieces by cutting the pile warp by sliding from one side of the loom to the other; this knife was curved. Later, a Monsieur Alsina replaced the original curved blade with a circular blade. Alsina himself built a loom in 1883 in which the wefts were inserted by two shuttles that moved simultaneously along the loom. Clearly, this new two-shuttle loom system produced twice the fabric of the original one-shuttle loom.

Once Barrau's patents expired in 1872, the new weaving and construction system was adopted in Germany, and as early as the 1880s the two companies located in Dulken, F. Tonnar and Jean Gusken, were manufacturing the first type of single-shuttle mechanical loom for velvet in double piece. In France, the industrial production of mechanical single-shuttle velvet looms began at the Beridot company in Voiron in 1880, somewhat behind what was happening in Germany, where the replacement of the hand-operated loom by the mechanical loom was almost complete. In the Lyon-Saint Etièn-ne-Tarare-Voiron regions, a great many mechanical velvet weaving plants for apparel were established during these years.

In 1901, when the patents expired for the construction of two-shuttle mechanical velvet looms, the Germans once again took the greatest advantage of the opportunity, promoting the development in Germany of a prosperous velvet industry, which is still extremely successful today, and is certainly one

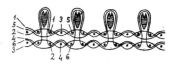

Plan of hand-made velvet in superposed double-piece technique.

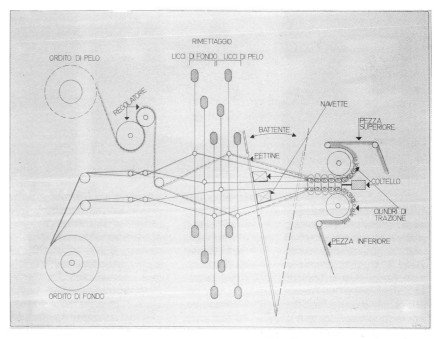

Plan for a modern two-piece velvet loom with two shuttles or grippers.

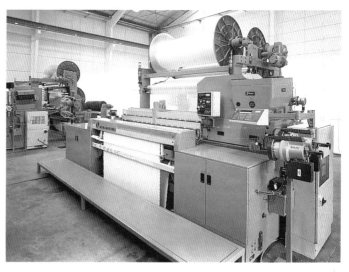

of the finest in the world. For the entire first half of the twentieth century, velvet looms continued to be manufactured, primarily in France, with single-shuttle models, and in Germany, with double-shuttle models. The best known French manufacturers were Beridot, Bicquert, and Marqui, while the leading German manufacturers were the Tonnar company and the Gusken company, founded in 1874, which was soon renowned for manufacturing the most advanced and modern of velvet looms.

The technology of velvet looms remained substantially unchanged over all of these years, while an increasingly refined execution was ensured, and new and more efficient devices were developed and refined, especially in the operation of the shuttle. During the early decades of the twentieth century, the production of mechanical looms remained largely centered in Germany and France, but an important manufacturing presence developed as well on the other side of the Atlantic, and the production of looms began in the United States as well, at the request of companies that had sprung up in the New World, modelled on their forerunners in the Old World. The mechanized manufacture of velvet, with the most modern looms, lowered the costs of production enormously, but after the first two decades, when the number of mechanical weaving plants grew very rapidly, the market for velvet underwent a brief crunch, and as a consequence, the loom manufacturers also were forced to halt operations unless they could radically renovate and improve their products.

The looms were not substantially revolutionized, but a continual and incessant process of mechanical upgrading accelerated the

The evolution of looms from the turn of the century to today. Models shown: Gusken and Van de Wiele.

growth in the efficiency of the machines, as well as improvements in the shuttle-launching device, and the mechanism of the cutting knife. An effort was therefore made to improve productivity, with the introduction of control devices for the loom, well suited to lighten the work load of the weaver.

The weft feeler and the warp guard were devices started in use, respectively, to ensure that the loom would stop operation once the spools ran out, or in case the warp end was broken.

The years following the war, up until 1965-1970, were largely a time of improvement of the shuttle loom. During these years, the first dobby machines were constructed for a double-shuttle loom two pieces face to face velvet, and the earliest experiments with the application of the mechanism for automatic spool changing for velvet looms. In reality the system of spool changing for velvet looms never quite caught on due to the complexity of the loom itself.

The Sixties were marked by considerable expansion in the use of mechanical looms, equipped with the insertion of wefts with rapiers, and in the end velvet looms made use of this extremely important advance in manufacturing. It was the Gusken company of Dulken that first presented in 1967 face to face velvet woven with rapier loom. This innovation, simple in principle, involved the insertion of two rapiers into the sheds of a face to face velvet loom in place of the shuttles, one for the upper piece and one for the lower piece. The rapier transports the weft yarn right to the center of the bolt (carrying rapiers) where another pair of rapiers (drawing rapiers) take up the weft yarn from the center of the bolt and draw it all the way to the opposite selvage. This device, the shuttleless loom, much as on ordinary looms for simple fabrics, made it possible to eliminate from the tasks of the weaver the cost of changing spools, which meant an increase the number of looms assigned per weaver.

Since in 1970, all manufacturers of looms have been working on this principle, and in a very few years, velvet shuttle looms have almost entirely disappeared from the scene, save for a few cases in which they are still in operation, for especially lavish articles.

The development of productivity in the mechanical loom over the last hundred years can be described as follows: from the loom of the late nineteenth century which performed at seventy to eighty RPM, with one shuttle and one loom per weaver, we have moved on to the more recent shuttleless loom built by Van de Wiele (Mod V M 22), microprocessor assisted, with speed of 350 RPM with two rapiers with weaver assignment up to fifteen looms or more. This change has meant that for a medium quality velvet, the production has shifted from half-a-meter per hour per weaver to 180 meters per hour per weaver and even more.

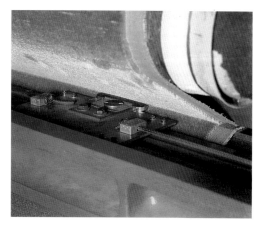

Weaving department in Lecco of Redaelli Velluti in a photograph taken at the turn of the century and another one taken in 1989.

The cutting of velvet. The knife sled produces the separation of the top piece from the bottom piece.

199

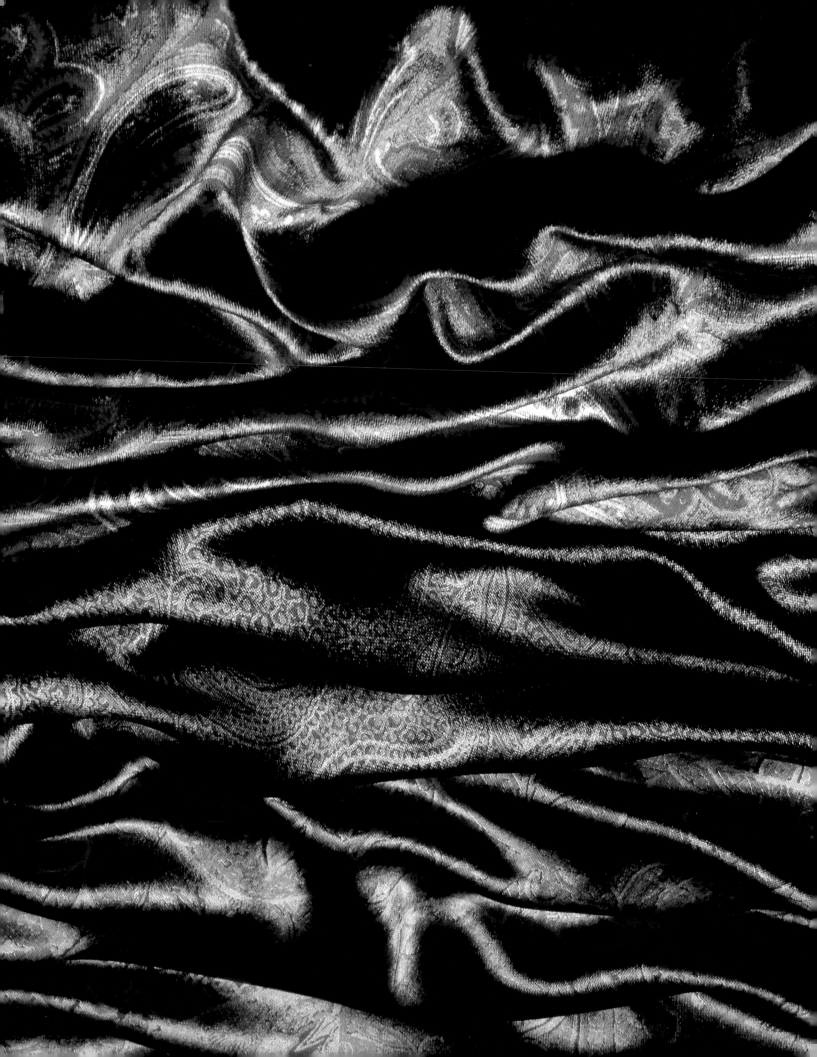

ASSOCIAZIONE COTONIERA
20126 MILANO

The Associazione Cotoniera was established in 1883 by cotton entrepreneurs and traders in order to deal with the matters strictly related to the cotton and allied textile yarns trade.

The Associazione Cotoniera gathers nowadays more than 280 firms, which cover 70% of the national cotton and linen sector.

The yelding fields covered are: spinning, weaving, finishing, linen division, sanitary material, sewing, hand knitting and similar threads, raw cotton agents.

The Association's purpose is to represent and to defend the common interests of the field: it mantains contacts with the competent national authorities and with central trade union organizations, it provides consulting and assistance to its members in tax and legal questions, in the foreign trade, in environmental matters, it provides a technical advice, studies and promotion services.

The Association, within whose framework a significant group of consortiums has been established, organizes specialized shows both for clothing (MODA IN) and furnishing fabrics (PROPOSTE).

The Association has cooperated to this unique work, in the frame of the velvet promoting activity.

THE ASSOCIATED VELVET MANUFACTURERS ARE:

COTONIFICIO CARLO BONOMI, 21013 Gallarate

DUCA VISCONTI DI MODRONE-VELVIS, 20060 Vaprio D'Adda

GASPARE TRONCONI, 21054 Fagnano Olona

LEGLER INDUSTRIA TESSILE, 24040 Crespi D'Adda

LIMONTA, 22041 Costamasnaga

MARIO SIRTORI, 22041 Costamasnaga

MOLTENI & C., 22045 Lambrugo

PONTOGLIO, 25037 Pontoglio

REDAELLI VELLUTI, 22054 Mandello del Lario

SCHIATTI F.LLI, 20030 Lentate sul Seveso

T.B.M., 21010 Besnate

TESSILE FIORENTINA VELLUTI, 50047 Prato

TESSITURA PIETRO CAZZANIGA, 22060 Bulciago

VIGANÒ, 22060 Nibionno

REDAELLI: ONE HUNDRED YEARS OF VELVET

Redaelli Velluti, the major producer of velvet in Italy, has its origins in 1893 when Alfredo Redaelli founded in Rancio, above Lecco, the weaving house, Velluti & Peluches, Alfredo Redaelli. He has studied and worked with weaving processes in Germany, France and was able to establish the first mechanized velvet weaving process in Italy. In 1912, after many trials, and successes, Alfredo Redaelli opened the Mandello Lario factory, to consolidate his position.

The traditions of the firm were retained by Riccardo, Alfredo's son, for a further 40 years, and continue today under the leadership of his nephew. All the experience of the early years and the constant updating of technology places the firm today in the forefront of production with outlets in fashion, furnishing, and industry. Clients such as Christian Dior, Ferré, Krizia, Ungaro, Valentino, Versace and Yves Saint Laurent, are well aware of the product quality. Alfa Romeo, Fiat, BMW and the Italian State Railways as well as the theatres of La Scala in Milan and Carlo Felice in Genoa use the function for their elegance, solidity and stylish confort. The products of Mandello Lario are distributed to all important international markets, including France, United States and Japan.